Time Out for Grief

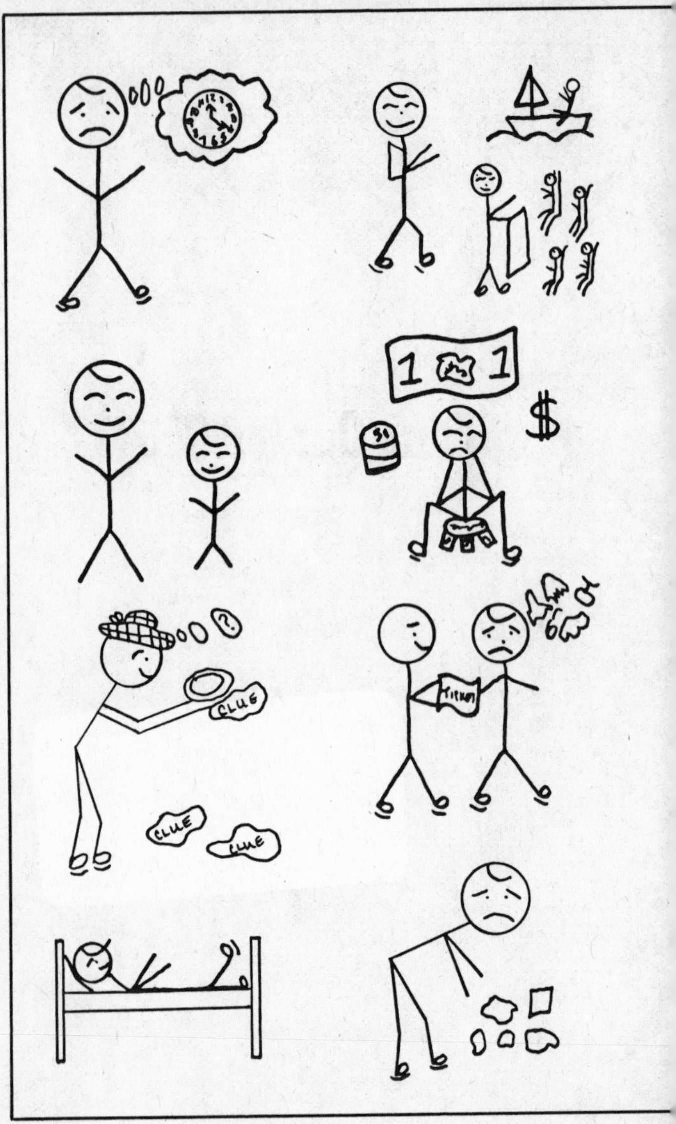

CLUE
CLUE
CLUE

Time Out for Grief

A PRACTICAL GUIDE TO PASSING THROUGH
GRIEF TO HAPINESS

Jean Gannon Jones

OUR SUNDAY VISITOR, INC.
Huntington, Indiana

An earlier version of this book was titled *For Crying Out Loud: How to Work through Grief to Happiness*

Copyright © 1979, 1982 by Jean G. Jones
REVISED EDITION
Library of Congress Catalog Card No. 81-85051
ISBN 0-87973-654-2

DESIGN BY PAUL ZOMBERG

Published by
OUR SUNDAY VISITOR, INC.
200 Noll Plaza, Huntington, Indiana 46750

PRINTED IN THE UNITED STATES OF AMERICA

To my daughters,
Leigh Ann and Jan,
who understood the need to write
of our experiences;
to my twin sister, Joan Ewing,
whose sympathy has never wavered;
to my sister, Sister Ann Patrick Gannon,
who helped me to laugh and to trust God again;
to my sister Nellie Thompson,
whose support and encouragement
saved me from a nervous breakdown;
and to all the rest of my family and friends,
who helped me through my own vale of tears
and encouraged me
to try to help others through theirs.

Contents

Preface

This book was written specifically to try to help the widow cope with grief, loneliness, and depression. But it applies also to others: the divorced, whose love has "died" and whose grief is sometimes more intense than that of the widowed; parents who have lost a child; the man or woman who has lost a sweetheart; the person who has retired or grown old and has lost a way of life.

For whatever reason we grieve, our individual problem and its resultant pain are overwhelming to us, and we must adjust to both. If you are battling loneliness and depression for any reason, insert your own problem wherever I speak of mine, and in that way, I hope, reading this book may help you to a happier today.

J. G. G.

CHAPTER ONE

Clues to Happiness

MOST OF US spend our lives searching for that elusive state called "happiness." We usually feel that we are about as happy as the next person, until a monumental problem comes our way—such as an incapacitating illness in the family, or divorce, or a retarded or crippled child, or a financial disaster, or an alcoholic spouse, or forced retirement, or the death of a loved one.

When we are confronted by such a problem, we can easily become deeply depressed and are likely to think we will never be happy again because the "problem" will not go away or is not likely to. Tragic circumstances, however, need not keep any of us from enjoying at least some of the good things in life *once we have worked through our grief.*

These following pages will probably surprise you if you have never had to face a tragedy in your own life. If you *have* done so, they will strike familiar chords inside you, because human grief follows certain patterns. When we grieve, our individual problem seems overwhelming to us, a feeling intensified by the fact that we have not learned how to work through our grief, or what kinds of behavior and feelings to expect in ourselves when we grieve.

I hope this book will help you work through your grief, so that you can return to a happy, satisfying life. I have written it specifically to help the widow; but much of what it contains applies as well to the woman who has experienced marital separation or divorce, and whose grief can be more intense than that of the widow. I hope that the book will assist also those women who are faced with, and must adjust to, other painful circumstances of various kinds.

Whatever it is that causes grief, grief causes predictable reactions and behavior in us. My case—the death of a spouse—is a common one; and, like most women in the same circumstance, I had no idea how to cope with it. No one could have convinced me, during the days and weeks after my husband died, that there was anything good left in life for me. I gave up hope of ever being happy again. I was living through a period of intense stress, and it took me some time to discover or re-learn that I did not have to be unhappy forever because of my widowhood or any other reason.

I eventually came through my grief a happier

person than I had ever been before, because I learned that happiness seldom "just happens"—we have some control over it. I discovered many techniques of behavior and thinking that *work* and offset the tendency toward negative thinking. These techniques can be useful to anyone facing personal tragedy. It is ironic to me, now, that the biggest tragedy of my life forced me to learn how to be happy even though I felt that there was nothing in my life to bring me happiness.

I felt that *my* life had also come to an end when Bob died, without warning, in April 1971. One morning, I was awakened by his cough, watched him raise himself up on one elbow and then slump down unconscious on the pillow beside me without uttering another sound. Twenty minutes later, at the hospital, he was pronounced dead—of a coronary occlusion. He was fifty years old. Only one week earlier, he had come to visit me in the same hospital, where I had just been operated on (hysterectomy). "We've got it made, Girlie," he said. "No cancer." We had it made all right—for seven days.

I was forty-five years old; our daughters, Leigh Ann and Jan, were ten and six. Bob worked for the U.S. Corps of Engineers, and I worked for the Veterans Administration Hospital. We were living in Bob's home town of Huntington, West Virginia, in the old family home, surrounded by our neighbors and friends, many of whom had seen Bob grow up. We were active in the Central

Christian Church and in St. Joseph Church, as well as in the Huntington community. Ours was a secure, comfortable, ordinary home that, within a half-hour period, became completely insecure, uncomfortable, and unordinary when Bob died, leaving me a widow, the girls fatherless.

Shock and grief took hold. The shock is what got me through the funeral. But grief tore at my insides day and night, left me limp and exhausted and unable to sleep. There was also a sense of horror that *this* could be happening at all.

I was glad to go back to my accounting job at the hospital, after two weeks of convalescent leave; but each day, grief and my attempts to shake it off were taking their toll. After a few months, just when I felt I was beginning to adjust to my new situation, I found myself waking up, morning after morning, shaking and terrified and unable to cope with simple tasks. I could neither eat nor sleep. My faith and trust in God changed to fear and a feeling of abandonment. My life had become unbearable twenty-four hours a day.

Finally, in desperation, I made an appointment with a psychologist for counseling. Bob's mother, elderly and in poor health, was our only relative in Huntington, so I had been thinking of moving back to South Dakota in order to be near my relatives, who could take care of the girls when I had the nervous breadown I thought was inevitable.

So the girls and I flew out to South Dakota that November, and I bought a house in Milbank, next door to my sister and her husband; I made definite plans to move into the house the following spring.

I hardly remember how I managed to sell the house in Huntington. Saying good-bye to "Grandmother" and all our friends there was unbelievably painful for the three of us. As we drove out of town, I concentrated on *not* looking in the rearview mirror; I did not want to see the city vanishing into the distance behind us. By then, I had begun to live as if what I was experiencing was in fact happening to someone else.

Now, whenever I pass the sign on Highway 77 that reads MILBANK 15 MILES, I recall how I felt when I first saw it in May 1972 and knew that Milbank, South Dakota, would be "home" for us, and that my life up till then lay forever in the past. The girls were excited by the adventure of moving, but I felt lost, afraid of the loneliness I saw ahead of me. At first, I was kept busy by arranging for the needed remodeling of the old house I had bought. I forced myself to meet people; and in the fall, I returned to work, as a nurse's aide. Yet I still was depressed much of the time. The ways in which I was trying to overcome the depression (I speak in more detail about those ways later) were not working; I was full of self-pity, which made me disappointed in myself. I didn't know that my attempts to adjust to grief were very typical, and that *failing is par for the course for everyone!*

A year after I moved, I began to make some headway. It was much easier to meet and see friends in a small town than it had been in a larger one; the children were happy; and all three of us were glad we had moved. I was busy at work and in social and church activities, and my life was moderately enjoyable and satisfying. I was still lonely, however, and felt it was impossible for me ever to be *really* happy as a widow. I felt that all I could expect was a continuation of that low-to-moderate level of happiness. Tension and depression remained close to the surface, and erupted in physical complaints that put me into the hospital with colitis two years after Bob died. Next I developed a severe back ailment that became increasingly disabling during the year that followed its onset.

During that year of my back ailment, I spent most of my time alone and in pain. I was forced to learn—finally—how to live with myself and to work at making some happiness *happen* regardless of my circumstances. As a result, after being operated on for repair of a ruptured disc, I began *honestly* to "love" life.

I think I would still be lonely and unhappy if I had not read everything I could find on the subject of grief or depression. I asked widows whom I knew what *they* had done when their spouse died. Sometimes I helped them in the process. Always, they helped me. Those who had moved through their grief to a full and satisfying life gave me hope for my own future. Those who had *not*, helped me even more, for they made me determined to overcome my tendency toward depression, and grateful for any progress I had made.

I discovered that there is no set "adjustment

pattern" for the widowed, and that with few exceptions it is a slow, tedious struggle to adjust to life after the death of one's spouse. This book is for the poor adjuster, like myself, rather than for the few who adjust rapidly. It is also for those with a negative self-image—which, I have come to believe, is a major handicap to adjusting to any personal crisis.

The techniques I collected for overcoming grief and depression *work*. My own problem was unexpected widowhood, and I deal specifically with that situation. But the same techniques work for any "grief situation." The techniques that I will discuss in the following chapters are steps on the path through grief to happiness:

1) Admit that you have the right to grieve over your situation, and allow yourself to cry about it.

2) Find understanding friends with the same problem, and share your feelings on a mutual basis.

3) Learn to like yourself (again) so that you can enjoy being by yourself for various lengths of time.

4) Change your negative attitudes about your situation and appreciate the advantages it has to offer.

5) Be on guard against destructive and painful bitterness and envy.

6) Trust God, in spite of normal negative feelings about Him after your tragedy.

7) Learn how to recognize the symptoms of

mental illness, and seek professional help if you need it.

8) Broaden your circle of friends and become involved in organizations and activities.

9) Take positive action to cope with financial problems.

10) Learn how to *make happiness happen* in your life, and laugh whenever possible.

CHAPTER TWO

Find a Friend Who's Been There

IN ANY grief situation, the first thing you must do is admit to yourself that you have a right to grieve over your problem, and allow yourself to do so. This can best be accomplished by finding a friend with the same problem, who also needs to grieve about it. Which puts me back with Peggy: in our first few months of emptiness and agony, we laughed and cried through together, right at the beginning of the nightmare, when even breathing hurt.

Peggy wasn't a friend who *had* been there. She was a friend who was *there* at the same time I was there—in as much pain as I was in, carrying that same gnawing feeling in her chest that I had in mine, that aching which never went away, day or night, when the lonely days went on forever and the nights were longer and lonelier.

The need for a special friend who will listen and

9

understand is primarily the result of the fact that our society does not permit people to grieve appropriately. For example: A man whose wife had recently died went into a restaurant with some friends. It had been only two weeks since his wife's death, but none of his friends mentioned her name. They all played the game I call "Pretend It Didn't Happen," following our society's unwritten rule: *The funeral is over; pretend the deceased person never existed.* Most people are uneasy about death. They avoid any mention of it either because they fear death, or because they do not know what to say to the bereaved.

I know of a young girl whose fiancé was killed in a car accident just before Christmas. They were to have been married on Christmas Day. She told her family later that all through the holidays she wanted to scream at them, *Talk about him. Why don't you talk about him?* But the family purposely avoided any mention of the boy, thinking that it would only make it harder for her to bear if they talked about him. The bereaved *must* grieve in order to get well. We must find someone who understands and who will permit us to talk out our grief. It is a matter of survival. Dr. John Brantner, a professor of health-care psychology at the University of Minnesota, has written that "sharing suffering openly relieves us of some of the burden."

People need other people in order to survive and be happy again. The loss of a spouse leaves a huge void that must be filled by others who care about us and for whom we care. Instead of sitting home alone and miserable, we must go out and make new friends who fit into our new way of life, if family and old friends do not.

Find *at least one person* who is in the same situation as you are so that you can share your suffering openly with one another. All through life, the difference between happiness and unhappiness generally depends on whether or not we have one close confidante to talk to frankly about our feelings and activities. It is particularly important to have such a friend during the severely stressful periods of our lives.

I was especially fortunate to find Peggy. Or did Peggy find me? She answered the phone about a week after Bob died, when I called our pediatrician for an appointment for some before-school shots for Jan, who was to start school in September. A mutual friend of ours had told Peggy of Bob's unexpected death just three days after Peggy's husband had died of a heart attack. So when I gave her my name, she said, "Say! I understand we're in the same boat. If one more person tells me they're sorry, I'm going to *scream*! Are you sick of hearing them say that?" I agreed I was, and within two minutes we were friends, sight unseen, and made plans to get together.

She was leaving with her three little boys in order to spend a few weeks with an aunt in Florida. She called me when she got back and came over with her boys the weekend following her return. We discovered we had much in common. She was younger than I, but we were both redheads, office workers, and mothers of young children. In addition, we both had a good sense of humor, which would "save" many a day ahead for us.

We were amazed at how similarly we felt about our situation. We shared numerous fears and feelings of frustration, reactions to well-meaning phrases that stung, ambivalence about even the smallest decisions, and feelings of unreality. We only brushed the surface that day we first met, but we both felt better and agreed to call each other often—and moan and groan some more. After she left, I recalled that we hadn't actually moaned and groaned much. We had complained, but we had laughed a lot more about our very painful situation. Just being able to *talk* about our situation with someone who understood had helped us to be able to laugh instead of cry.

We both felt funny about being seen out in public together; so we saw each other on weekends, usually with all five kids; but we called each other every day and became increasingly frank with each other about how miserable we felt. We discussed our "hang-ups" and made fun of the ones we didn't share, but admitted that our own were just as ridiculous. We upbraided one another for putting things off that needed doing, and for our lack of interest in doing anything at all.

She sympathized with me for not being able to eat. I sympathized with her for eating compulsively. She had a boat to sell. I had a car to sell. We pushed each other into selling them. We complained bitterly about toilets that ran all the time, televisions that stopped working, vacuum-cleaner belts that broke, and lawn mowers that refused to start. We gave one another sympathy, but we also told each other—loud and clear—that we had to learn to live with the situation because we didn't have any other choice in the matter. Then we'd laugh like maniacs, as though that was hilariously funny!

One of us was usually "up" when the other was "down," so we could generally lift each other out of the blues; but sometimes we would both be blue at the same time, too blue even to cheer ourselves up.

On week-ends we took the kids on hikes or to the amusement park, or out for pizza. We also went to the cemetery together, as our husbands were buried within a short distance of one another in the same cemetery. Once, after I had been out of town, she called and told me she had put a sprig of holly on Bob's grave and didn't want me to worry that some girlfriend of Bob's had put it there. We laughed to the point of tears about how funny it would have been if after twenty-four years of my not worrying about "another woman," I'd have to start now!

The beautiful part of a friendship like this is that each of you understands all the problems and pain involved in your situation *without having to explain them.* There are so many things that cannot be put into words—things that other people cannot understand, no matter how hard they try or how much they care about us, *because they haven't been through what we are going through.*

Peggy and I were lucky to be going through it all at exactly the same point in time. We felt that a woman who had been widowed for even six months would have forgotten how bad it was at first. We didn't know then that no one gets over it that fast. Having a friend who has experienced the same problem at close to the same time is very important. The reason is simple. I remember how terrible those first months were, but, like having *had* an abscessed tooth, I am not feeling the pain now. Being in the same age-bracket as your friend also helps, but is not all-important. We hurt at any age.

Peggy and I felt more comfortable with one another than with most of our family and friends, whom we so often felt expected us to be braver than we were. We talked about how much we hurt, cried when we felt like it, and laughed whenever we could about whatever we could. We moaned about the fact that we felt as though the whole world had deserted us. We couldn't believe how insensitive people could be. A co-worker of Peggy's found her crying at her desk a few weeks after her husband died and asked her what was wrong. She yelled, "Just everything, that's alll"

When we took our kids to the Ice Follies and laughed and ate popcorn, we both knew how heavy the other one's heart was, and how much we wished our men were there with us instead. We knew how angry we both felt at the world and everyone in it who was happier than we were, and how hard we were battling to keep our sanity. We drank gallons of coffee together and said the same things over and over about how we felt inside. How she felt at quitting time, when her husband used to pick her up. How I felt when I sat in Bob's recliner, which we used to sit in together. How we each felt when we woke up in the middle of the night and reached out and found emptiness where our husbands should have been.

On our good days we congratulated ourselves and one another, and on our bad days we told each other tomorrow had to be better because it couldn't be worse! Like kids, we applauded one another's feeblest efforts to adjust to the strange, lonely world that we had been forced into and that we despised. We admitted to each other that we were horribly afraid, afraid of being alone, afraid of what lay ahead, afraid that life would never be good again without someone to love.

Peggy was there for me at the very first, when I needed her the most, when family couldn't be there, and when old friends didn't know how to help. I helped her, and she helped me. That's what friendship is all about—a two-way street. Later, when she began dating (as I didn't), we had less and less in common and we gradually drifted apart as she moved back into the "couple world" and I began seeing other single friends. She married again and moved away; and our friendship now consists of an annual Christmas card. For a time, however, ours was an all-important, beautiful friendship in which we demanded nothing of each other except understanding and caring.

It was a stroke of luck for Peggy and me to have found each other. Today, it doesn't take any luck to find a friend "who has been there." Support groups for the widowed and the divorced can be found in almost every town in the country, where you can find friends of all ages who understand and care. We have such a group even in our little town, and it's exciting to see the friendships that develop and the healing that comes about when people help one another through the pain and grief of a common problem. In large cities, there are support groups for just about any personal problem. If you cannot find a group, call someone you know who has the same problem, and explain that you'd like to talk about it. The person will be glad you called.

Talking over feelings and problems with people who understand your situation is entirely different from talking to relatives or friends who have no way of knowing what you are going through and cannot imagine the problems involved. In the case of a spouse's death, it is especially hard to talk to others. Dr. Virginia Van Coevering, a clinical psychologist in Mesa, Arizona, who teaches courses on adapting to widowhood, says that "society is uncomfortable about facing death. Some people will even walk across the street rather than talk to a widow." Because people do not know what to say to us, or how to handle grief situations.

So we must choose friends who will understand our situation, and often have to find new friends. Making new friends is not difficult *if you sincerely want to make new friends.* All through life, we should be constantly making new friends to replace those who move away, or die, or are lost to us for one reason or another. Unfortunately, we are often too particular about who we will permit to be our friend, judging people by a false set of social values, consequently overlooking gems; and at the same time *choosing* to remain lonely. Michel Quoist, in *The Meaning of Success,* compares people to buses. Like buses, many people "are all filled up with themselves. They have neither time nor space for those waiting to get on." Yet if we let them into our lives, our loneliness will vanish.

Don't underestimate the value of any friend. Friendships make the difference between a full life and an empty one, whether you are married or single, young or old. You will be amazed at how exciting and interesting life can become when, in addition to your family and old friends, you make room in your life for new friends *who understand.*

Abraham Lincoln was a friend who understood what grief was all about. Of his four sons, one died in infancy and another at the age of twelve. To a grief-stricken friend, Lincoln wrote:

In this sad world of ours, sorrow comes to all. It comes with bitterest agony. Perfect relief is not possible except with time. You cannot now realize that you will ever feel better. And yet this is a mistake. You are sure to be happy again. To know this, which is certainly true, will make you some less miserable now. I have had experience enough to know what I say.

You may already have friends in your same grief situation. I know a woman who lost her husband and whose best friend's husband died six weeks later. Young widows often have a difficult time finding other widows their age, but older widows will help. One very young widow went to a support group of older widows a month after her husband died and cried when she told them that her mother objected to her dating "so soon." She got the solid support and sympathy of everyone there and was told to live her life *her own way*, and was given concrete ideas about how to go about it.

If *you* do not have a friend who's been there, *find one*. Get together and laugh—and cry—and complain. It's a matter of survival.

CHAPTER THREE

Who Says Thoroughbreds Don't Cry?

SHORTLY after Bob died, a friend came up to me at work, patted me on the shoulder, and announced in a bracing voice, "Thoroughbreds don't cry, you know." I assumed he meant: (1) thoroughbreds don't cry; (2) if I was a thoroughbred, I would not cry; and (3) if I *did* cry, I was not a thoroughbred. I controlled the impulse to tell *him*: (1) *his* spouse had not just died, so (2) he didn't know what he was talking about, and (3) he could go take a long walk on a short pier!

This is a good example of a friend who hadn't been there but who—as I appreciated better later—was trying to help, but said the wrong thing. It takes courage, and caring, for our friends to say anything at all to us after the death of a loved one, so don't get upset if they say the wrong thing to you. We did too, before it happened to us. Don't get upset at them; but don't follow bad advice, if they give it, either.

This was one of the first sources of bad advice I was given in my first years as a widow—along with, thank God, much helpful advice. I have sorted it all out (primarily by trial and error, by myself and others) and will help you recognize the differences so that you can act on the good advice and not waste your time on the bad!

For a starter, thoroughbreds *do* cry. And so do commoners, and so does anyone else with blood in her veins cry when she loses a loved one. Unwittingly, famous people have done a great deal of harm in recent years by their public stoicism in the face of death, causing us to identify that type of behavior with courage, and fostering the idea that crying is undignified and cowardly.

This misconception is extremely unfortunate, because masking our grief and bottling up our emotions can be physically and emotionally dangerous. There is no disgrace in showing grief. It is a perfectly normal human reaction when you lose a loved one or grieve for other reasons. It is actually abnormal *not* to cry under such circumstances, and is often a sign that the person is living in a state of shock.

When in shock, people perform like robots, without emotions. It is a frightening experience, an eerie feeling that is totally against human nature. When in shock, we *want* to cry; we *feel* like crying; but we cannot cry. We walk and talk like ourselves, but we feel as if we are standing in a corner watching someone else in our shoes. The someone else is a robot called Shock, who automatically takes over when our feelings become paralyzed in a situation too traumatic for us to be able to comprehend until later.

When in shock, a person may even appear to be more competent than usual. I marveled at the composure of a friend at the funeral home where her husband was being waked. Four months later, I was marveling at my own composure in the same situation, even though I had a reputation for crying easily. I have trouble remembering names and frequently cannot recollect the name of a close friend; yet I never forgot a name when greeting people, some of whom I scarcely knew, at the funeral home. The robot was doing its thing.

The period of time a person remains in shock varies. The first deep period of shock lasts anywhere from two or three days to five or six weeks. Partial shock can last for months, in some cases for more than a year. One woman told me she felt she was in partial shock for almost two years. Others claimed they "walked around in a fog" or "didn't know what was going on" for months.

You will do "just fine" in shock, and cry very little. After the shock wears off and reality begins to seep in, however, you will feel like crying at the drop of a hat—particularly if the hat belonged to your late husband! If you play it smart, you will leap out of shock in a hurry, because immediately after the funeral, mild signs of grieving are considered appropriate (even *admirable!*) in our society. Shortly after that, however, our euphoric so-

ciety frowns on grief. You will notice friends looking uncomfortable and changing the subject if you
so much as mention your husband's name. And
tears are an absolute no-no.

I was getting desperate and beginning to think I
must be a weirdo for not "shaping up" as society
obviously expected of me a few months after I was
widowed, when a friend gave me Granger Westberg's little book, *Good Grief.* Westberg quickly
convinced me that I was not going crazy—a common fear among those experiencing grief—and
informed me that there were several stages people
go through in any grief situation.

Showing emotion is one of the grief stages that
Westberg lists. He tells us: "We should allow ourselves to express the emotions we actually feel.
The person who holds himself tense, who refuses
to let go, may be in for trouble."

Two seemingly easy rules to go by are: (1)
Don't cry if you don't feel like it. This is simple,
because crying isn't great fun and is actually hard
to do if you do not feel the urge (unless you are a
good actress). The second one is not as easy as it
sounds: (2) *Cry when you feel like it.* It is indeed
easy to cry when you feel like it, and actually
takes a great deal to effort *not* to cry if you feel
like it. The problem (alas and alack!) is that it is
not always convenient to cry because it is seldom
"appropriate" in our society to do so. So we bottle
up our tears until we are alone, or postpone them
indefinitely. Either tactic usually results in emotional or physical problems.

Much of the reason why grief is so hard to handle is the fact that most of us have been taught not to show our emotions. From childhood on, we have been told: be brave and keep a stiff upper lip; crying is a sign of weakness; tears don't help any; self-pity is despicable; crying embarrasses people; crying upsets the children; laugh and the world laughs with you, cry and you cry alone; nobody likes a cry baby; crying isn't polite; and so on.

Forget what you've been taught against crying. God gave you tear ducts to use when you needed them. Jesus cried openly for Lazarus. Viktor Frankl, a Jewish psychiatrist who spent years in a Nazi concentration camp, does not look down on tears. In *Man's Search for Meaning,* he writes piognantly, "There was no need to be ashamed of tears, for tears bore witness that a man had the greatest of courage, the courage to suffer."

Once you come out of shock and the floodgates are open, you will feel as if you can't stop crying. It is during this period that many make the mistake of forcing themselves to stop crying for one reason or another, often supposing that it will hurry the grief process if they stop. Instead, the process slows down.

After the initial shock wore off for me, I started crying buckets, but I made the same mistake others make and quit crying for all the wrong reasons; I put on a happy face, and lived to regret it. After counseling, I stopped fighting my feelings, rode them out, cried appropriately for Bob, and so began my long journey through grief.

Gradually tears will cease to serve a purpose for you emotionally, and you will stop feeling the urge to cry anymore. Until you are cried out, however, *do not stop crying.* If you do, you may end up having a nervous breakdown, or with temporary paralysis. It can, and does, happen. Tears bring relief, so whenever you feel like it, *cry!*

CHAPTER FOUR

Pick Up the Pieces and Start Over

RABBI Joshua Liebman has written that "every new stage of life is a shattering one emotionally and forces us to build some new adjustment out of the broken fragments of our past, out of the precious shards of earlier molds" (*Peace of Mind,* 1947).

Marriage is the closest of all human relationships. The death of a spouse is therefore considered to be the most stressful of any of the life changes that occur during a normal lifetime. If you have been widowed, all the king's horses and all the king's men cannot put your old life back together again; so you have no other choice than to pick up the pieces and start over.

In the first months of widowhood, every new day is a challenge during which you will be faced with so many adjustments that they will make your head swim. Just making it through each day will take effort no one else will believe. So don't expect too much of yourself; but don't give up, either, because you will slowly but surely begin to live and enjoy life again. The widow's typical first mistake is to assume, along with the general public, that "time will heal" rapidly. This is a preposterous assumption, considering the magnitude of her loss and the complete change wrought in her life. Healing, for her, is necessarily a slow process.

We hurt so much at first that we barely function, and drag through each day. If you are a new widow, I want you to know that "drag" is the best anyone can do under the circumstances; and that even though it may not seem like it at the time, *you are making progress in working through your grief even if you have only sat and cried all day.* The fact that you haven't committed hari-kari proves you are courageous, and puts you one step forward at the end of the day. I am not kidding when I recommend that you visualize a huge neon sign on your bedroom wall flashing YOU DID SWELL! at the end of each day, even if you sat and stared ahead of you all day. You have to get your feet on the ground before you can begin to walk alone.

Shock helps us escape grim reality for a time, but as we gradually comprehend what has happened, life becomes increasingly painful. Since husbands and wives do so much together, everything will remind you of the past. Every stick of furniture, love songs, comments, the garage door, the leaky faucet—all will bring back memories. Which is why Scarlett O'Hara's technique of "thinking about it tomorrow" doesn't work. We have to face our grief and deal with it constructively *today.*

The sooner your life gets back into a regular routine, the better. It will *not* get back to "normal." That's the big problem. You must get used to a totally different life, one that will seem *abnormal* to you for a time.

I was anxious to get back to work after Bob died, because I thought that once I got back to my desk, my life would seem more "normal" and I would be able to get my mind off his death. I found out that grief doesn't work that way. The harder you try to get your mind off your problem, the harder it is to think of anything else. We are very seldom able to think of anything else at first. This, too, is normal grief, and your grief *work* consists of *keeping on trying.*

Never stop trying to be happy

We *must* keep on trying to get over our grief. When you are experiencing grief, you find that it is difficult to think at all, much less concentrate. But you can develop techniques that will eventually help you get your mind off your grief. Don't become discouraged if these techniques do not work at first. Every time you *try* to use them, you are learning and coming closer to succeeding. It's like hitting the keys on a piano. In order to learn how to play the piano, you have to sit down at the piano and *try* to hit the right keys, or you won't ever learn. To acquire any skill takes months, even years, of practice; and bungling is part of the learning process.

If you are depressed for any reason, you must keep on trying to be happy in spite of that reason, or you will never be happy. Developing a happiness-oriented outlook will take practice. So you should start practicing *right now*.

Try to enjoy the "right now"

My counselor once told me it was a proven fact that a person cannot think of two things at once. I would now be prepared to argue with him, because when I was not consciously thinking of my problem, the *feeling* of grief was there. For instance, if you were carrying a refrigerator on your back and someone stopped you and told you that you had just won the Irish Sweepstakes, you would forget the refrigerator and think about all the money you had won, but you would still be feeling the weight of the refrigerator.

Our grief becomes a part of our very being, a feeling of sadness that sometimes will not go away even when we are "enjoying ourselves." We can be doing something that is enjoyable and takes concentration—like playing cards or tennis—and still have this awareness of "things being all wrong." One woman said she'd find herself laughing and wonder to herself, "Why don't I feel happy?"—then remember why, and go back to trying to forget.

Trying to forget your problems and enjoy life, at least a part of the time, is your objective. In *Death Be Not Proud,* John Gunther tells of his teenage son's bravery while dying of a malignant brain tumor. As he went to bed one night, the boy told his mother that it had been "another fine day." He did not wait for a tomorrow that might not come to be happy. He enjoyed what he could out of every day he lived.

He was an exception to the general rule, however, for very few people appreciate the happiness that comes their way each day. Dr. Maxwell Maltz (in *Psycho-Cybernetics,* 1960) claims that unhappiness is largely a habit, and that most people "do not live nor enjoy life now, but wait for some future event or occurrence" to be happy. "They will be happy when they get married —when they get a better job—when they get the house paid for," and so on.

We widows are tempted to postpone living and enjoying life until we stop missing our husbands; and until then we *think we are not living and enjoying life at all, but merely existing.* We are not alone. Look around and you will see multitudes of people who do the same thing. This postponement of happiness is tragic, because it makes the difference between the happy people who love life and live it zestfully, and the people Thoreau referred to when he wrote that most people "lead lives of quiet desperation."

You have a good "reason" for living a life of quiet desperation *if you choose to do so*; but I as-

Live for today [handwritten marginal note]

sume you want to try to be as happy as possible instead—*right now*. Don't wait until "tomorrow" to be happy. Enjoy what you can this minute, *today*.

If you are making plans for the future, think in the *now*. If you are ordering tickets for the theater next month, have some recorded music or a radio station playing and a cup of coffee at your elbow to enjoy while you write the check out for the tickets *now*. When you are getting gas for a trip the day before you go, talk to the attendant and appreciate what he has to say about the roads and the weather *right then*. Don't wait until you leave on your trip or get to the theater, to live and be happy. Tomorrow may never come, so enjoy what you can of the present, even if only for a few minutes at a time.

When we are depressed, a few minutes at a time is much easier to handle emotionally than thinking—and worrying—about the years to come. As Michel Quoist advises:

Why do you keep putting off until tomorrow the life you have to live today? One of these days there will be no tomorrow, and you won't have gotten around to living your life at all. Perhaps you cling to memories of the past. But that was yesterday, and today you can't do a thing about it. The present is of such short duration that you don't take much notice of it, yet it alone counts because it alone is in your hands. In fact, the whole of your life is simply a succession of pres-

ent moments. The present moment is delicate.
Handle it with care. It provides only a narrow
passage; there is no time to worry. It passes quick-
ly, so it won't tire you out (The Meaning of Success, *1963*).

Train yourself to think in present moments, not
in the (usually dreaded) future.

Make some happiness happen

In *How to Be Your Own Best Friend,* Mildred
Newman and Bernard Borkowitz state:

People say they want to be happy, but they ex-
pect happiness to happen to them. They don't see
it's something they have to do (today). We must
realize that we have a choice; we are responsible
for our own good time. We would much rather
blame someone or something for making us feel
unhappy than take the steps to make us feel bet-
ter. (Right now.)

When tragedy strikes, we have a justifiable
"something" on which to blame our unhappiness;
but unhappiness is painful, so we must take steps
to make ourselves feel better. The problem is that
generally we have no idea where to begin to try to
be happy.

You can't wave a magic wand and be happy,
but you can begin *trying* to be happy. You are the
only one who has control of your life and your
thoughts. How do you feel about starting to try to
be happy right now? You have a miserable day

ahead of you—lonely, empty, full of grief, right? It can't get worse, can it? So any little bit of happiness would be an improvement, wouldn't it? It's *easier* to sit and do nothing and feel miserable, granted. Maybe this is one of those days when you will do well to hold your head up instead of hiding it under a pillow until bedtime.

If you can, however, try to *do* something to make your life a little brighter. I don't mean something grand and glorious. Having a cup of coffee with a friend would be a small plus instead of a minus, wouldn't it? So phone a friend and ask her to come over; don't wait for her to call you. If you are absolutely miserable, a few minutes with a friend would be that many minutes during which you would be slightly-less-than-miserable, right? So call.

Afterward, you may tell yourself it only made things worse. You hate women, and she talked about her husband a lot and made you miss your husband all the more. She called you a widow and said, "Time will heal," and you felt like belting her one—*but inviting her over was a step forward anyway*. Remember, she wanted to help, even if she didn't know what to say. So what if it wasn't *great* fun; the truth is, nobody can make you feel good right now, except your by-this-time *very* "late" husband, who (let's face it) is not going to show at all. He cannot be here, so somebody else will have to do.

Sitting and pining aren't the answer. Anybody is better than nobody; so try again. Call another friend to have lunch with you tomorrow; go for a hike. Get out and do *something*. Anything is going to be an improvement over being alone and miserable. "Our choice is between grief and a full life. To take the first steps toward that life may be painful, and you may have to endure sharp pangs of loneliness and loss. But you were lonely anyhow . . ., so what you are losing now is only a dream" (*How to Be Your Own Best Friend*).

You must work at making your life happier when you are home alone too. Learning to live with (and like) ourselves is a very big part of our adjustment—a particularly difficult part for most of us.

Here again, adopt the attitude of *trying* to enjoy what you are doing. It may take a great deal of effort to adopt that attitude because you have probably lost all interest in doing anything without your husband around to share the results of your efforts. Remember, it is your *attitude* that matters. I have seen many a widow work like a beaver at painting, papering, cleaning, or gardening in an attempt to get her mind off her troubles; but because she made no attempt to *enjoy* what she was doing, she got the job done *but did not make herself any happier*—which is our goal.

It is terribly difficult to think and live in the present when your thoughts keep going back to the past. Early in my grief, I attempted to get my mind off the past by cleaning out dresser drawers. I went at it with exactly the wrong attitude of: "Woe is me, I'm really unlucky to have to be cleaning out this drawer now that I don't have anyone to do it for me." (Which was a ridiculous thought, because Bob never cleaned a drawer out in his life except when he was looking for golf tees or his Army discharge!)

I cleaned out drawers every evening after dinner, and at least I had the sense to admit to myself that this routine filled in some empty hours and made me feel better when I foresaw that at least now I would be able to open a drawer and find what I was looking for. It certainly wasn't "happiness," but I was living in the *now* and inching ahead through my grief. In retrospect, it is interesting that I chose to clean out drawers, which I had always despised doing, rather than sewing or doing something else I enjoyed doing; it definitely shows now negative my thinking was.

Anything is better than thinking sad thoughts. Read. Watch television. Do fancy needlework. Garden. One man said he planted the largest garden he had ever had in his life the year his wife died; and he worked in it from sunup until sundown. If you are a gardener, you know he enjoyed it in spite of himself. Many widows work through their grief and enjoy themselves at the same time by doing fantastic pieces of needlework.

Adjustment to single life after having been married for years does not come easy. It is probably the hardest work you will ever do in your life. The most difficult thing about it is that, without being aware of doing it, we fight against adjusting. This resistance is natural, however, because we did not *want* to change our lives. We chose to make many of life's changes, such as going to college, moving, getting married, or changing jobs; but those situations could always have been changed if we had wanted to change them. The fact that our situation now is totally irreversible is one of the reasons why it is so terribly traumatic for us.

So while we are telling ourselves we *must* get used to this new way of life—and working hard at doing so—at the same time we are subconsciously telling ourselves that we do not want to have anything to do with our new way of life, *because we hate it.* This attitude, of course, makes working through our grief and making a fresh start (at our age, yet!) that much more difficult and discouraging.

So discouraging, in fact, that many people give up trying to overcome their depression—like alcoholics who give up trying to stop drinking, smokers who give up trying to stop smoking, and fat people who give up trying to stop overeating—because the trying takes so much effort, and they get so discouraged when they keep on losing the fight *that they stop fighting,* feeling it is useless even to try anymore.

Do not ever stop trying to overcome your grief. Don't even settle for "accepting your lot." Aim at learning how to be *happy* in spite of your situation. With the necessary effort, you can come through your grief to a good life—happy in a way different from what you knew with your husband.

Your life will be happy in a different way because married and single are two totally different ways of life with entirely different problems. You like being married and hate being single; so getting used to being single will take time. You *will* get used to it and enjoy life again, however, if you are willing to exert the necessary effort to change your habits *and* your attitude toward your situation. Being single is not "all bad," anymore than being married is "all good." Begin right now to get into the habit of "feeding" yourself positive thoughts about your single life whenever you can, rather than always thinking of the negative aspects of it. You can concentrate on the disadvantages to your life at any time during your lifetime, or you can concentrate on the advantages to your life at that point in time.

You can purposely choose to make it your practice to think of the good things left in life, or you can purposely choose to dwell on your problems and loneliness. Get into the habit of thinking positively about your life whenever possible. Also get into the habit of enjoying whatever you are doing.

I scraped five coats of wallpaper off my downstairs walls, and people think I'm crazy when I tell them I enjoyed doing it; but it's the truth. I did a wall at a time, played the stereo, took countless coffee breaks, and stopped whenever something more interesting came along.

Gardening for some people is a fantastically engrossing hobby, but to me it looks like back-breaking manual labor. Reading a book is hard work for some people; other people can't keep their noses out of books. Baking for many women is a fate worse than death, but others are happy as a lark baking up a storm. It's all in our *attitude* about what we are doing.

When we are depressed, getting anything at all done, much less enjoying what we do, is a major problem. Even the necessary jobs don't seem worth doing; in addition, it is difficult to remember what needs to be done.

Daily reminder-lists are a must

I learned the value of reminder lists years ago. When you are a working wife and mother, you *have* to be organized. My lists became more important than ever after Bob died, because I forgot things easily, couldn't concentrate, and lost all motivation to do anything at all. My reminder lists now began to depress me, however, for two reasons.

My sister Evelyn discovered the first reason for me when she came for a visit and I told her my lists upset me. With sisterly love and caring, she said, "I know what your problem is without even *looking* at your lists. Any fool knows you don't put too much on a list!" She went on to explain that when she got everything on her list done, she felt great, and when she went over into the next day's jobs, she could feel "downright smug" about them.

This was clearly half the trouble. The other half

I discovered myself. My lists *did not include any fun things.* I wasn't making any happiness happen.

So I got smarter about making up my lists. I made them shorter and included some planned fun; and my lists helped me on my way to making a new life for myself.

Daily lists will help you put your new life into operation and will reflect *your* priorities of work and play (no longer your husband's). Some examples might be:

At first: 1. *Bathe, dress, comb hair, brush teeth.*
             2. *Fix meals.*
             3. *Phone a friend.*

Later: 1. *Write some thank-you notes.*
             2. *Do the laundry.*
             3. *Go over to a friend's for coffee.*

Later: 1. *Bake cookies.*
             2. *Go out for lunch with Gwen.*
             3. *Shop for groceries.*

I suggest you make a long list of appropriate (for you) AT HOME and AWAY activities. Choose *one* or *two* items from each list every day. As you feel better, add more items to your daily list; but remember, *any fool knows you don't put too much on a list!* You will know yourself how long to make each day's list.

Ideally, your lists will eventually include involvement in community and social organizations, as well as short- and long-term home projects. But at first your lists should not put you under any pressure. The following are some unpressured AT HOME and AWAY suggestions to get you started planning your days of work and fun.

AT HOME	AWAY
Bake a cake	*Visit a neighbor*
Wash a window	*Go shopping*
Read the paper	*Go to a show*
Clean closet shelf	*Dinner with a friend*
Write a letter	*Go to church*
Ask a friend over	*Go for a hike*
Clean refrigerator	*Go for a drive*

Whether you are *at home* or *away*, be aware of everything that is going on around you. Grief deadens the senses, and they need to be reawakened. By making lists and following them, you will accomplish the following objectives:

1. You will become less absorbed with your grief.

2. You will improve your self-image by getting the necessary jobs done.

3. You will acquire the habit of making some happiness happen.

4. You will live in the present, not in the past.

5. You will develop a happiness-oriented outlook and style of life.

Beware of alcohol

So many people resort to alcohol to ease the pain of their grief that I feel a word of warning is required. I didn't have to talk about this problem with grieving people—it was obvious that many widows I knew were using alcohol as a crutch. For years, men have commonly used liquor as a cure-all for their problems; and now more and more women are following suit.

In moderation, drinking can be a good, relaxing, and pleasant thing to do; but drinking can also be dangerous, *particularly solitary drinking,* and should never be used as an "escape" from your situation. "Escape drinking" can quickly turn you into an alcoholic.

Liquor may enable you to forget your problems temporarily, but it will make you more depressed than ever the next day; so you will be strongly tempted to keep right on drinking. Instead, you should make a strong attempt to *face* your problems and do something constructive about improving your situation, instead of faking happiness temporarily, and tempting fate, by "leaning on the bottle."

Alcohol addiction is on the rise at an alarming rate in our country. Heaven knows you have enough problems already without multiplying them a hundredfold by becoming an alcoholic. So limit your drinking, or you could become one of the alcoholism statistics.

Let the bells ring

You can train yourself to overcome your grief and depression gradually, by *refusing to answer* "bells" you have subconsciously trained yourself to respond to painfully. You have all heard of Pavlov's dogs, which salivated automatically at the sound of the bell that announced their dinner. When we first lose a loved one, every time that person's name is mentioned or we think of him, we experience pain. *This reaction is normal.* At first, songs hurt, books that mention husbands or lovers hurt, comments about husbands hurt, seeing "whole" families in restaurants makes us cringe at the presence of the empty chair at our table. These things are bound to hurt at first. The hurt is actually a part of the healing process and serves a definite purpose. The *danger* lies in letting yourself continue to react automatically with pain after that pain stops healing. In other words, *do not let it become a life-long habit to react to your circumstances with pain.*

The object of this technique is to try not to be sad when you are reminded of your husband, even though you have "reason" to be. Try not to answer the "be sad" bell. It's just like not answering the phone when it rings. You can hear it ringing, *but you do not have to answer it.* You have a choice in the matter.

You tend to react a certain way out of habit, and let people and circumstances "dictate to you how you shall feel and how you shall react. You are acting as an obedient slave and obeying promptly when some event or circumstance signals you to—'Be angry'—'Get upset'—or 'Now is the time to feel unhappy' " (*Psycho-Cybernetics*).

When you are reminded of your husband, your

emotions will signal you to "be unhappy." This is normal; but when you can, tell yourself instead, "I have a right to feel unhappy, but I would prefer *not* to feel unhappy." Tell yourself how you *want* to feel; don't become a victim or slave of your circumstances.

In *Between Parent and Child,* Dr. Haim Ginott presents this same principle in an example of a mother's typical reaction to a child's spilling milk at a meal. The mother will get upset and shout at the child, "How many times have I told you to be careful?" Yet mothers do not *have* to answer the "get upset" bell. Instead, a mother could calmly hand the child a cloth to use to clean up the mess. Sometime in our life, however, we have been taught that we *should* get upset over spilled milk. The idea that we do not need to make a fuss over it comes as a surprise—as surprising as the fact that we do not have to answer the phone when it rings, or that we do not have to answer a personal question when someone asks us one.

We do not *have* to react in any particular way. We can decide *how* we want to react, and train ourselves to react *in that way.*

Here is another example of how this principle works: I went to a party where the hostess seated all the widows together, assuming that we had much in common, but bruising my sensitive-widow image. My first reaction (answering the "bitter," "inferior," and "be sad" bells) was to say to myself, "Are we outcasts even among women?" I had already answered all the bells, true; but after I admitted the hurt, I *chose* to let go of the hurt and have a good time. Sometimes we cannot avoid getting hurt; but we *can* avoid nurturing the pain, which is sadistic.

You will be amazed to find that, with time and practice, you will not only stop answering the bells, but you won't even hear them ring!

On your mark, get set, . . . start!

During the first terrible months after Bob died, I identified my lot with that of a woman in a nursing home who said to another, "The days are long, aren't they." Her remark spoke volumes. Our days are long because they are without the person we loved. It is difficult to motivate ourselves to fill our empty hours because very little matters to us when we are depressed, and because grief and its resultant depression sap our energy. Energy creates energy, so it is important to get into motion—which brings us to another technique that overcomes inertia. (Inertia applies to people as well as to objects.)

Newton's law of motion is: "A body in motion tends to remain in motion, and a body at rest tends to remain at rest." The depressed person not only tends to remain at rest, but tends to remain totally immobile! So the trick is to talk ourselves into *starting* to do something—anything —and let the law of motion work for us.

Force youself first to do some small job. The idea of doing a big job will exhaust you before you even begin. Promise yourself that you will quit if you want to in ten minutes, but *start*. Decide to sew for ten mintues, or read the paper, or straighten up the living room, or wash a load of clothes, or go to the store for milk. Decide what you are going to do, *and then do it.*

Setting a timer will make you feel better about the task, because you are not going to want to do it at all. Starting is the hard part. Once you get moving, you will probably do more than you agreed to do—the whole wash instead of one load. Even if you stick to the agreement, however, you will feel better because you will be amazed at how much you can accomplish in ten minutes and will like yourself better for having accomplished *something.*

When jobs stack up until you have dozens of things that need doing, you don't know where to start. The secret, again, is to *start somewhere!*

One day I was running around in circles because I had too many things on my list that *had* to be done that day—tomatoes too ripe to postpone canning; a luncheon date I didn't want to miss; laundry that had to be done because we were out of jeans and underwear; a stencil I'd promised to type for a teacher; and a meeting of my bridge club that night. A friend had stopped for coffee and stayed too long. When she left, I felt so pressured by my list that I began to feel depressed. None of it seemed worth the effort it was going to take me. I also knew from experience that when I backed myself into these corners, I could end up with a migraine headache.

I rationalized that if I got a migraine, I'd get *nothing* done, so I sat down and drank another cup of coffee as though I had all day to drink it, told myself that I couldn't possibly get everything done, but that I could get some of it done if I started doing it.

I checked my list and decided the laundry had the highest priority, so I gathered it up and sorted it first; from then on; the laundry did itself, because my washer and dryer are right off the kitchen, and it took me five seconds to pop loads in and out when the bells rang. Then I typed the stencil and dropped it off at school on the way to lunch. After lunch, I decided to can as many tomatoes as I could that afternoon and throw the rest of them out. I ended up getting them all canned because I was no longer tense about it, and because once I got into motion, things got done in a hurry. A body in motion tends to remain in motion—*even me!*

Don't be afraid of change

None of the techniques I have mentioned will work very well when you first try them. Your life has changed too drastically for anything to work for a while. Just remember that everything is constantly changing in this less-than-perfect world of ours. Circumstances have changed before, and they will again. Agreed, widowhood is one of life's biggest problems, but we had problems before. Life will never be the same again for us, but that is not to say it can't be good. All through life, we move from one stage of life to another, and each stage has its own set of joys and sorrows.

Being a child wasn't all happy. As teenagers, we had problems as well as good times. Being newly married wasn't all sweetness and light—there were big adjustments we had to make, along with the fun; and rearing children isn't all fun or all hassle. Each of life's situations falls far short of bliss. It is our ability—or inability—to adapt ourselves to and then enjoy the present *in spite of its problems* that will make or break us.

We widows are apt to tell ourselves we would be happy if our husbands were alive. We would then be telling ourselves something only partially true. Were we always happy when they were living? (If you said yes, you are either a big liar or you have a poor memory.) Look around at the married couples you know. Some of them are happy, but some of them are not. The father of a friend of mine was a minister. He said one of the most heartbreaking problems he met with as a counselor was "married loneliness." Many married people also have "good reasons" for not being happy. They feel unappreciated, unloved; their lives are boring; they have financial problems or problems with their children; they are old, sick, and so forth.

Even if you were unhappy before your husband died, however, you felt secure in a familiar way of life—which is a mighty big plus compared to afterward, when you do not know what is in store for you and feel uncomfortable in an unfamiliar way of life.

Madeline Gray, in *The Changing Years*, writes that "most of our fears are merely the fear of the unknown. We are so sure security is the main answer to life that we blindly hold on to a known way of living even when it's bad. But if we somehow find the courage to push ahead and do the thing we are afraid of, then the new life may turn out to be ten times better than the old." We are so insecure in our new way of life and so afraid of the future that we panic and become incapable of handling the present moment. You can deal with today *and enjoy yourself* if you stop worrying about tomorrow.

When I decided to move, I went into cold sweats thinking about packing all the boxes, selling the furniture, selling the house, getting the stove and dryer disconnected before the moving van came, and moving away from all my friends. But when I told myself, "I just have to pack a few boxes a day, I don't have to think about anything else today," I got along fine.

The same thing worked before I had my back operation. I'd shake like a leaf if I let myself think about how I'd manage if I ended up as an invalid and had to build on a downstairs bedroom and find someone to come in and take care of the kids *and* me. But if I just thought about what I had to do *that day*, I found I could cope fairly easily.

Changes can be difficult to adjust to, but changes can also bring exciting results. Many widows say that being alone is the hardest thing to adjust to. But being alone plays an important part in one's becoming a whole and happy person. "An adult often needs aloneness to grow, to get to know herself and develop her powers. Someone who cannot tolerate aloneness is someone who doesn't know she's grown up. Genuine growth means having the courage and confidence to try new things and in the process to let go of the old ones" (*How to Be Your Own Best Friend*).

Letting go of a known way of life is not easy. The good times are few and far between at first. Savor them. Make them last longer by avoiding thoughts that will bring your grief back to smother you. The good hours will gradually turn into good days, until finally the sun will shine most of the time. It will never shine again in entirely the same way, but life may be brighter than it has ever been before because with practice you will learn to appreciate what you have right now, and will no longer postpone happiness until a "perfect" tomorrow—which *never comes for anybody*.

After I had been widowed eight months, I wrote in my journal: "I am finally able to look ahead. The fact becomes plainer every day that I don't want to leave the past behind but that I must do so if I am ever to be happy again. No matter how much I want it not to be, that part of my life is gone forever." I was using many of the techniques I've mentioned, and all the willpower I could muster, but I could not overcome my deep depression. I not only didn't go forward, I kept slipping backward. Then I would decide I must not be trying hard enough, and would try harder and fail some more—until I was ready to scream.

Those first months, the harder we try not to think of our loved one, the more aware we are of his absence. The harder we work at trying to be happy, the unhappier we become. I had no patience with my failures; I expected too much of myself; and today I constantly see others making this same mistake.

Learning to accept failing is a major part of coping with grief. You cannot fail *if you are not trying to win,* so failing in itself is proof that you have the courage to keep on trying. Forget your failures. Keep reminding yourself of the times you win. Think of yourself as you are in your happier and more enthusiastic moods. *You will help yourself feel that way more often.* If you think of yourself as you are at your unhappiest, you will make yourself more depressed.

Make the most of it when you are feeling chipper, but don't be surprised when you fall on your face. *Expect* to fall on your face—then it won't be so hard on you when you do! When you are depressed, don't get discouraged. Tomorrow will be better. Everybody has highs *and* lows. No one goes on high all the time.

Continually keep in mind that if you are trying at all, *even when you lose,* you are picking up the pieces and building a happy new life for yourself.

CHAPTER FIVE

Think First Class!

THIS CHAPTER won't make any sense to you if you have a "healthy" self-image. Unfortunately there are very few people who have completely healthy self-images. Most of us have sick-unto-dying ones! The typical widow feels inferior because she is a widow, and is sometimes even ashamed of the fact, because of our society's prevailing attitude toward the single woman—an attitude that makes going from being a married woman to being a single one an automatic put-down (except among young people).

Soon after we are widowed, most of us begin to feel we are looked down upon and discriminated against. Lynn Caine, in her book *Widow*, claimed that widows are treated like second-class citizens. Regardless of how *you* are treated, *you are a first-class person*. Don't ever forget it. *Think first class*, because if you think you are a second-class person, you will be one. "For as a man thinketh in his heart, so is he" (Proverbs 23:7).

You must develop a good self-image *as a widow* in order to be happy as a widow. That destiny made your life miserable was unavoidable; that you should intensify your misery by developing an unrealistic self-image is tragic and foolish.

It isn't easy to develop a good, realistic self-image under the best of circumstances, of course, much less as a widow. Why do so many people suffer with poor self-images? God only knows, but it is obvious that a low self-esteem causes millions of people untold heartaches. Part of the reason is the fact that today's media have led us to believe that only young, slim, good-looking, intelligent, witty, and wealthy people count in this world. We do not all fit into that mold, but each of us is beautiful in our own way, with individual personalities and talents that only we can give to others. So why are we generally dissatisfied with ourselves?

Why do I feel inferior because I'm not a gourmet cook? Why does a woman I know, who *is* a gourmet cook, feel inferior because she has never held a salaried job? Why does another woman, who is a perfectionist in her home and on her job, feel inadequate because she never attended college? Why does a man I know, with two master's degrees to his credit, feel inferior because he was raised on a farm? As I said before, God only knows! I haven't figured it out.

A friend of mine who is a paraplegic helped me see the unnecessary grief we lay on ourselves by clinging to unrealistic self-images. He is a brilliant, interesting person, but he doesn't appreciate his own worth. He didn't choose to be crippled, anymore than I chose to be widowed; and being crippled or widowed doesn't make anyone more or less a person. In both situations, we might feel that society looks down on us as "excess baggage," and that we are restricted socially. Far worse than society's attitude toward us, however, is the fact that we ourselves often adopt that same attitude toward ourselves.

In India, outcasts cannot walk on the land of the higher castes; they must walk in the ditches. The most pitiful part of the situation is not so much the fact that they are made to do so, *but that they themselves feel* that they are unworthy to walk on the land of their "betters." Many people you know have self-images just as "sick," however. We ourselves may feel we are too fat or too short or too tall or too ugly or too poor to be "as good as" someone else. We consider ourselves inferior because our skin-color or religion is "wrong"—or because we are not married.

It took me a long time to develop a "good" self-image. I didn't have one *before* I was widowed, and I put myself down even more afterward. I drank too much at a class reunion, to ease the pain of being the only one there who had to stand up and say, "I am a widow." At that time I still felt that being a widow, particulary without an escort, made me inferior.

My daughter Jan finally woke me up. She was

ten at the time and came home from school at noon crying. When I asked her why she was crying, she sobbed, "Because I'm fat." I couldn't believe my ears—she not only was *not* fat, she was too thin! I asked her what made her think she was fat, and she bawled, "Because the kids keep telling me I am."

It was not one of my more patient days. I took her by the arm and marched her to the mirror in the entry hall and ordered her to look into the mirror and *see* if she was fat. I snapped, "If you're fat, Jan, *you're fat*; but if you are not fat, the kids can tell you that you are all day long but that will not make you fat!" I added, "You're fat, all right, Jan—*fat in the head*"—and I sent her back to school.

I was furious at her for being so stupid. Then I suddenly thought of my own "poor widow" image. I had thought of myself as inferior because I was listening to what society was telling me: that I was not "as good as" a married woman. I had to admit that I was a much bigger fathead than Jan was, *because I was old enough to know better*. That incident really opened my eyes, and I stopped being furious with Jan and got furious with myself. How could I have been so idiotic? I had a mirror, didn't I? I had some smarts, didn't I? I might not be a superior person, but neither was I inferior.

Right then I decided I was as important as anyone else, and ever since then I've had a good self-image. I have a sign in my kitchen that says:

"When you're as great as I am, it's hard to be humble." Friends who didn't know me before can't believe I used to have an inferiority complex, and my own family says I'm a different person.

I'm a first-class person—even if I'm not married. Why should being married or single have anything to do with a self-image? Nuns and priests don't feel inferior because they are single. Why should we? It's all in our attitude about ourselves. Society does sometimes make us feel like outcasts when we become widows, but that doesn't mean we have to fall into the trap Jan fell into and consider ourselves outcasts. The same thing is true in feeling you are a "fifth wheel." If you don't let yourself feel as if you are one, you won't be one. If you see yourself as a worthwhile person and an asset to a group, that is what you will be. If you accept yourself—as you are —others will, too.

Dave Adkins is a perfect example of how self-imaging works. He has an artificial arm with a hook on the end of it, but Dave is not *disabled* because of it. *His loss of an arm has not hurt his self-image.* He doesn't wear his "like real" hand; he wears shortsleeved shirts so you can see the hook and the whole apparatus. He doesn't hide it. He'll take if off and hand it to you if you drop something, and say, "Here, use this." There's a sign in his office that reads: "Don't think of what you have lost, think of what you have left." Dave is active in sports and in the community. No one ever thinks of Dave as handicapped, because he isn't. But if *he* thought he was, Dave *would* be handicapped. Dave has accepted himself exactly as he is—and so has everyone else. He's a guy with a hook for a hand—the same guy who used to have a hand where the hook is now.

Appreciate yourself exactly as you are. You are a woman who has lost her husband—*the same woman you were before you lost him.* Accept yourself as a widow; don't be ashamed of your widowhood or feel inferior because of it. You should feel proud of yourself for coping with the problem involved.

It is hard for us to accept ourselves as widows, but the truth is that not many of us accepted ourselves before we were widowed. Actually, not many of us knew ourselves well enough before. Few people do know themselves well. Once we get to know and like ourselves, loneliness no longer has control over us.

Experts agree that everyone experiences loneliness at times, because each person is basically alone and isolated within himself or herself. Chronic loneliness, however, stems from a low self-esteem. Holding a low opinion of yourself is not a virtue. Appreciate yourself for what God made you—a remarkable person with abilities you have yet to discover.

Jess Lair, in *I Ain't Much, Baby—But I'm All I've Got,* says each of us has only what God gave us to work with and that we all pretend to be something we are not because we are afraid people won't like us the way we are. Widows imagine that others do not like them because they are widows. We also have an identity problem, because women's identities are usually immersed in their husbands' identities in our society. So much so that when we are widowed, we each lose our "identity" and must develop a new one as an individual. While this is a difficult task, it is rewarding when you accomplish it. God made each of us with different personalities and talents; and being proud of our specialness is a marvelous feeling.

No two people are exactly alike, not even identical twins. My being an identical twin made my struggle for an individual identity after Bob died all the more difficult, because I had *never* had an individual identity. People couldn't tell Joan and me apart when we were girls, and we grew up assuming that no one really cared which was which! We both answered to "Twin" most of the time—our identities immersed in one another's. After I was married, my identity became absorbed into my husband's, so until he died I had always been half of a pair. No wonder I found it hard to train myself to say "I," as my counselor instructed me to do. I had been a "we" all my life, and I had no idea how to go about being an "I."

I had a tough time "becoming an individual" in my own right, but I *love* being one now. Moving helped me because it gave me a personal identity, even though it was one I hated at the time: "Jean Jones, widow." To my surprise, I found that instead of the "half a person" I felt I had become after Bob died, as a single I gradually became a completely whole person for the first time in my life.

Years ago, people used to give a widow an individual identity of sorts by referring to her as "the Widow-So-and-So." I thought of that when I became widowed and cringed at the thought. Now I feel that having been known as "the Widow Jones" would have been a good thing. Everyone would have known that I was a widow without my having to explain it, and I would have accepted my identity as a widow faster and not been ashamed of it.

There will always be people who are smarter, kinder, prettier, wittier, and more capable and considerate than each one of us, I'm sure, but I have to be me, and you have to be you—we have no other choice—*and we are each great in our own way.* You owe it to yourself to learn to know and like yourself. Someone once asked Katherine Hepburn if she ever got lonely living by herself, and she said she never tired of her own company! She knows and likes herself.

Our best friend is our self-image. "It is the strength of your self-image which, by and large, will determine whether or not you can overcome your obstacles. If you have accepted an idea—from yourself or from any source—and are firmly *convinced* that idea is *true*, it has the same power over you as the hypnotist's words have over the hypnotized subject" (*Psycho-Cybernetics*). So if you have accepted the idea and are firmly convinced that widows are lonely and miserable, you are hypnotized, and you will have to dehypnotize yourself from those negative thoughts or you will continue to be lonely and miserable.

In the United States, approximately ninety percent of adults over the age of twenty-five are married, so *not* being married makes widows "different" in our society; and that which makes people different often makes them feel inferior. Different is not necessarily bad, of course. Men usually like being tall, yet I once worked with a man who hated being tall. He got his height early in life and had always been "too" tall for his age, and he still felt uncomfortable about being "different," even though many other men envy him his height. Dave Adkins, with his hook, made his being different something beautiful. Some people even capitalize on being different—like Yul Brynner, who made baldness enviable.

Women often tie their self-image to the way they look. The happiest women, with the healthiest self-images, don't care too much about how they look, however. During a television interview, Katherine Hepburn kept running her fingers through her hair until it looked like a rat's nest. Her hairdresser was probably crying in the wings, but Hepburn didn't care how her hair looked. Her self-image didn't require that she have a perfect coiffure.

Some people set up certain requirements to prove to themselves and to others that they are worthwhile people. The use of good grammar, for instance, or getting a college diploma, or being a terrific bridge player or golfer. All are excellent goals in themselves, but our *reasons* for setting ourselves such goals can be sick, and a sign of a poor self-image. If making a mistake in grammar or looking bad on the golf course can ruin your day, you have a poor self-image. If you need *proof* that you are as good as someone else, you don't really think you are that good! You don't have to prove yourself to yourself. Start now to accept yourself as someone good and worthwhile in and of yourself.

The movie *On the Other Side of the Mountain* retells the true story of Jill Kinmont, who broke her neck skiing as a young girl. It wasn't until she accepted herself as a paraplegic that she was able to make a happy new life for herself—and she didn't do that overnight. We cannot accept ourselves as widows overnight either. We have to move gradually into our new life. Don't let your self-image suffer because you think you are not adjusting as fast as you "should." Remember that no one knows the problems you are facing *except you*. Not even another widow knows how hard your individual adjustment is, or how hard you are trying to cope. Don't put yourself down for any reason.

Eleanor Roosevelt said, "No one can make you feel inferior without your consent." If you feel you are inferior to another woman because she is married and you are not, then you might just as well be inferior. Society will eventually "open its doors" to single people, *but not until we appreciate our own worth.*

The most encouraging aspect of my association with widows and divorced women is to watch them adjust and increase their ability to cope. It is terrific to see women who never drove a car or managed their finances before, develop confidence and use talents and abilities they have never tapped before—and feel good about themselves in the process.

Men have a far easier time adjusting to widowhood than women do, because men have been taught to be independent; women, on the other hand, have been taught to be dependent upon men. In *Self-Assertion for Women,* Pamela Butler catalogs an amazing number of self-defeating attitudes that have been drilled into women from birth—attitudes that promote depression. It is usually necessary for us to "deprogram" ourselves of false ideas we have been taught about women's capabilities and strengths before we can move ahead *independently happy,* in control of our own lives and happiness—loving, caring about, and needing others, but not emotionally dependent upon them.

Don't confuse a good self-image with conceit. Having a good self-image just means recognizing your own self-worth and abilities and feeling good to be the person you are. One of these days, if you don't already, you will really feel good about yourself *as a widow.*

Once you learn to be independent and happy in

spite of your problems and obstacles; once you learn to deal with your life the way it is rather than the way you would like it to be; then you will have no one but yourself to blame if you don't regard yourself as a first-class person.

CHAPTER SIX

Where Are You, God?

ON THE WAY to work one day, early in my grief, I shouted out in the car, "Where are you, God?" I felt He had deserted me when I needed Him the most.

Most of the people I went to for advice attended church regularly, yet one of the common stages they had gone through was a period when they blamed God for "doing this to me." One man said he stopped going to church for more than a year because he was so angry at a God who would do such a thing to him. He interpreted his wife's death as "God's will" in the sense that God purposely inflicted this hurt upon him. The very expression "God's will" seems to have the connotation of bad news for many, rather than the "good news" it actually is. Don't be surprised if you feel that this cross you now bear is His "fault" and temporarily resent Him bitterly.

One of the comments the bereaved get tossed at them is: "God never gives you a cross you can't carry." Peggy and I saw red every time someone said that to us. We felt that God had obviously miscalculated our strength.

Many of the people who shared their deeper feelings with me had experienced frustration in their relationship with God and with religion in general after the death of their spouses. They felt abandoned by God, were upset by their inability to pray in a normal fashion, and went through a period when they "hated" God and had guilt feelings about their hatred. I never hated God, but I was afraid of Him for a long time—which was just as illogical a reaction.

We all have trouble praying when we are deeply depressed. I found it almost impossible to pray after Bob died, because it hurt so much to pray. A friend told me not even to try to pray, that God would understand—which he would, of course. No one understands what we are going through as well as He does, or cares as much as He does.

In looking back, those of us who had difficulty with more formal prayer for a time felt we were actually using a higher form of prayer at first when we beseeched Him desperately throughout the day: "Just get me through this hour . . . let me sleep and stop thinking . . . my God, don't let me cry here in front of everybody. . . ." Gradually, praying in your usual fashion will cease to be a problem and will once again become a source of consolation for you. You will probably resort to prayer more often than ever before, however, and experience a new comfort from prayer.

Many of us wondered why, if we really believed that God loved us, we felt "worse than ever" in church and couldn't keep from crying, particularly at Communion time. We came to a logical conclusion. We had two completely different responses to sympathy from others. We felt *nothing* when people offered sympathy out of a sense of duty, but at other times, *when we knew the person really cared*, even though the person said nothing, just squeezed our hand, we felt like crying because we sensed their love and sincere sympathy. And who cares most about us? Who knows exactly how much we hurt, what we are going through, and how difficult it is for us? God. If you are blessed with faith in God, you know how much He loves you and will feel His love and sympathy in church—and the knowledge will bring tears. Good friends understand tears, so don't hold them back with God or any of your other good friends. Tears heal.

If there is ever a time in our lives when we do not know where we are going, it is after the death of a spouse, because all our plans are torn asunder. Years ago, when I was on a trip with my sister Patricia, we ran into a bad snowstorm and could hardly see the road ahead of us. Pat told her kids, "Say a prayer that God gets us there safely." A few seconds later a little voice from the back seat chirped, "I asked God to get us there safely, but God said, 'Where?' " Father Joseph McCoy of the Marianists, in his little book *After Winter*, writes: "It is possible, in the midst of loneliness, to obey the summons to move ahead when you don't know where you are going. It is possible to find God in the dark." This is precisely what we do when we are grieving. We obediently move ahead blindly, day after day, without the slightest idea where we are going. Rest assured, however, that God knows *exactly* where you are going, and has plans for you even though you have none of your own. Trust Him. His plans will bring you closer to Him, which in turn will bring you happiness and contentment. Unfortunately, trusting God is hard to do under any circumstances, and becomes particularly difficult in a time of adversity.

Trusting God *sounds* so easy! So why do you suppose it's so hard to do? Trusting God means letting go of the reins, letting Him take care of things. Trusting God means believing that "His will" is what is best for us. The trouble is, we don't want to accept God's will unless it is the same as ours! It's like good advice. Someone said: "The trouble with good advice is that it usually interferes with our plans." We all know that trusting God works, because we've seen it work in our own lives and in the lives of others, but we find it hard to let Him be in control. We want to help Him do things, *our way*.

Trusting God is what I do after I go through the above routine and have loused things up by "helping" God do things "my way." I finally get tired of trying to run the show, and actually *do* leave things up to Him, even if I don't do it gracefully. I tell him, "I'm *really* going to leave things up to you now, God, because you can't make a bigger mess out of things than I've made." Am I actually testing Him? Maybe I am saying, "Let's see you get me out of *this* one!" And of course, He does—beautifully.

Things work out like magic, and each time it happens, I tell myself that I'll always trust Him after this. I honestly intend to, but then I get all involved in the next problem, and before I know it I am back trying to handle things on my own. I get it all mixed up with "standing on your own two feet" and "the Lord helps those who help themselves." When I get myself backed into a corner again, I panic and let Him take over.

Part of the problem is that the Lord doesn't speak to me as loudly and clearly as he does to people who are closer to Him than I am. But lately I think I have gotten a lot better at listening. Now I know that He always answers my prayers, even when what happens isn't the way I wanted it to work out. I have found out that His "answer" is always *what is best for me.*

I'll probably never get close enough to God to trust Him all the time, but God knows I'm working at it. Someday I hope we'll all get smart enough to stop beating our heads against the wall and admit we can't do anything alone, and start depending on someone a lot smarter than we are (God) to run our lives for us.

I have another reason for wanting to get closer

to God. I have noticed a direct relationship between a deep love of God and happiness. Some people associate piety with folded hands and a long face, but I've found the exact opposite to be true. The most religious people I know are the busiest and happiest people I know.

Blue Cloud Abbey is an Indian Mission at Marvin, South Dakota. We go to church there occasionally, and afterward the monks invite everyone to share rolls and coffee with them. The monks are busy, happy men who joke and laugh a lot. They relax and let God run their lives; the results are an inner peace and joy that shows. They are busy from sunup until sundown, but never too busy to stop what they are doing when others need them. They love God, people, and life—and they radiate happiness.

Another example of a person close to God is a woman who is the happiest, most carefree person I know. She is seventy-some years old and lives alone. She lost everything she owned in a fire not long ago, but the next day friends saw her clicking down the street in her high heels as happy as a lark. She's made a habit of accepting what comes as God's will, and trusting Him to know what is best for her. She is gradually going blind, but she never seems to have the time to be worried about it. She lives in a small two-room apartment without a private bath and doesn't have a car or a color TV, but she enjoys every minute of every day. And if you're lucky enough to be around Issy, you'll enjoy every minute too, because she is an extremely intelligent, exciting, joyous person. She prays a lot, laughs a lot, and worries about nothing. She leaves everything up to God.

Speaking of God and religion includes how we feel about death, and life after death. Our society doesn't talk much about God, much less about death or a life after death, until death strikes close to home.

Most of the people who have helped me through my grief are Christians. And Christians believe in a life after death. It came as a surprise to me, then, to find that many of these same people were clearly reluctant to talk about life after death. It seemed they *believed* in life after death; they just didn't want to *talk* about it. Talking about it made them feel insecure and frustrated; and their ideas, for the most part, were vague and often contradictory.

One woman felt her husband had "no conscious life as we know it here," but would not say exactly what kind of a life she thought her husband did have. Another woman said. "Well, of course you don't know what's going on after you are dead." This remark floored me, because I have always had exactly the opposite idea about life after death. At funerals we pray: "For your faithful (who have died), O Lord, *life is changed, not taken away.*" Someone wrote: "Death is not extinguishing the candle; it is putting out the light because the dawn has come." In that changed life, instead of *not* knowing what is going on, we will finally find out what *is* going on! We will finally know all the answers. We've been told all our lives that "God's ways are not our ways," and I, for one, am dying (forgive the pun) to find out what His ways are all about.

For instance, how do you suppose God will explain why "life" isn't fair? As soon as I reach those pearly gates, I'm going to start asking questions. Why are some people born rich and others poor? Why are some people born smart and others stupid? Why are some people born beautiful and others homely? Why are some people born healthy and others crippled physically or mentally? Why are some couples parted by death when they are young, and others not until they are old? These questions have frustrated me all my life; I can't wait to find out the answers to them—and a great many others!

I've heard sermons that made heaven seem terribly boring. I'm convinced that heaven is really a terrific, joyous place to be, with the kind of action each of us enjoys. I'm convinced also that we will be not only *conscious* in Paradise, but also aware of everything going on in this world too. I'm sure our husbands are waiting for us in that new life of theirs where there is no pain or loneliness, and that they are in the company of exciting, witty, intelligent, beautiful, good, kind people who give love to, and receive love from, one another.

I'm sure Bob is aware of what is happening to the people he loved in this life, and that he still loves us and always will—just as the children and I still love him and always will. *Because love nev-*

er dies; love is forever. In some beautiful way I can't explain, I feel closer to Bob now, and love him more, than I did when he was living and minor irritations and life's problems got in the way. Someday the pain of separation will be gone for you, too, and just the warmth of your husband's love will remain with you, *forever.*

Many women I have talked to have felt this closeness. One woman wrote me, "I felt like I didn't ever want the sharp pain to go away because then it would mean I had forgotten Tom. But that isn't true. I know now that one never forgets. I feel Tom knows about the kids' and my accomplishments and that he is proud of us for having made a good, happy life for ourselves without him."

Another woman said she definitely thinks her late husband knows what is going on in this world and told me she went dancing one night with a friend who asked her to waltz. She said she almost told him she couldn't waltz because her husband had always told her she couldn't waltz, but decided to let her friend find it out for himself—and to her amazement she didn't miss a step. When she got home that night, she said she told her invisible husband, "You big dope! For thirty years you told me *I* couldn't waltz, and all the time it was *you* who couldn't waltz!"

My idea of heaven didn't change much after Bob died, but my idea of hell did. I remembered a TV show I saw in which hell was described simply as a place without love. I thought of that show because, after Bob died, I felt as if there wasn't any love left in the world. The man in the show found himself in a room filled with people, but he was all filled up with himself and his needs and he didn't know how to love anyone else, and they were the same kind of people and didn't know how to love him. They were all in a hell of their own making—a place without love.

In the first months of bereavement, many people described their pain in the same way: "This is hell." Contrary to the people in that TV show, we know very well what it is to love and be loved. Grief numbs the senses, however, and the loss of our spouse's love is so catastrophic that we temporarily lose our ability to love others, or to care about the love of others for us—which temporarily puts us in a place without love. Because we feel we have lost our husband's love, and because we cannot feel the love of others, it is no wonder we think, "This is hell," and feel terribly sorry for ourselves.

Some people will tell you self-pity is a sin. *Not true!* Self-pity is *human.* Christ felt pretty sorry for himself in the Garden of Olives and on the cross. He wanted to skip the whole business, just as we would like to do. He, of all people, knows and understands how we feel. How can anyone believe that God, who is *all* love and *all* goodness, is going to blame us mortals for being human? He made us, so He understands our weaknesses better than we do. He knows all about our struggles to overcome our self-pity. He knows all about how alone and unloved we sometimes feel. So He patiently waits for us to be able to give and receive love again—and then our hell is over.

That day in the car, I knew God was near but I could not understand why He wasn't helping me, why He was letting me struggle on alone. The answer was simple. He wasn't letting me struggle on alone. He was always there making sure I got the help I needed. Later I was able to look back and clearly see His hand guiding friends and circumstances to ease my pain.

For instance, there was the Sunday afternoon when I was sure I couldn't stand the loneliness another minute and some friends "happened" to stop by with their kids, to take my two girls and me for a drive in the country.

Then there was the worst weekend of all, before I sought counseling, when I felt I absolutely could not cope, and my brother-in-law "happened" to see a sign on a trip to Lexington that said "Huntington 100 miles," and he "happened" to suggest that he and Joan and the kids drive over to see how my kids and I were doing.

Still later, Joan "happened" to suggest that I move back to Milbank, where we had grown up. I was at first irritated that she would even suggest such a thing and didn't consider that I loved Huntington. But she'd planted the idea, and I gradually began thinking about its advantages. When my daughters and I flew to South Dakota to consider the wisdom of moving there, the old house next door to Les and Nellie, another sister and her husband, just "happened" to be for sale, and just "happened" to be in my price range, and I just "happened" to like it—even though I am fussy about houses, requiring them to have some "personality" before I can get interested in living in them.

At the time each of these things happened, I just thought it was lucky, or coincidental. Now I know it was neither. God loves us dearly, and helps us—directly, through prayer, and indirectly, through people. *Trust Him.* For a long time, I was unable to pray; I was too busy just trying to hold my head up. But He knew I needed help, and He saw that I got it. He had plans for me even when I didn't have any of my own. *He has plans for you.* Just let Him push you where He wants you to go.

People told me that, years after they lost their spouses, they could look back and see how God guided them through the darkness, helping them to move ahead when they didn't know where they were going. Jobs opened up. Chance acquaintances dropped casual remarks about the very thing they were worried about and made suggestions that helped them make the right decisions. They met people unexpectedly (just as I met Peggy) who helped them and who became important in their lives. Sooner or later, we all came to understand that *no one ever struggles on alone.*

Tragedy often teaches people to trust God. Years ago my father told me that the best thing that had ever happened to him was his bank's going broke in the 'twenties, "because," he said, "it taught me that Someone Else was running the show, not me, and that I had to depend on Him." We also find that we are not in control of our lives and that we have to depend on God to guide us to happiness. Sandwich prayer into your day. God will never fail you. Ask Him for help even with your small problems; tell Him your needs and thank Him for His blessings; and you will be given the strength and guidance you need to cope with your problems, the love you need, and the peace and happiness you yearn for.

God is love. Think of love as a lighted match. Our married love was a bonfire of love; but if we could gather enough matches, they could make an even brighter flame. Once you reach out, you will find yourself interested in and loving others, and they will love you. We may not be loved in exactly the same way we were loved before, but it will be the same commodity. Kathleen Norris wrote, "Man's love is fire, and mother love is pain, but sister love is sweet on earth as rain."

All love is terrific. *It is the best, the happiest thing that life has to offer.* Trust God, and He will light your life with His love—through prayer, and through people.

In my darkest hours, the following prayer by Cardinal John Henry Newman gave me consolation and hope:

God has created me to do Him some definite service; He has committed some work to me which

He has not committed to another. I have my mis-sion. I may never know it in this life, but I shall be told it in the next.

I am a link in a chain, a bond of connection be-tween persons—He has not created me for naught. I shall do good; I shall do His work. I shall be an angel of peace, a preacher of truth in my own place while not intending it—if I do but keep His commandments.

Therefore I will trust Him. Whatever, wherever I am, I cannot be thrown away. If I am in sickness, my sickness will serve Him; in perplexity, my perplexity may serve Him; if I am in sorrow, my sorrow may serve Him. He does nothing in vain. He knows what He is about.

He may take away my friends. He may throw me among strangers. He may make me feel desolate, make my spirits sink, hide my future from me—still He knows what He is about.

CHAPTER SEVEN

Give Me a Ticket
on a Plane Crash, Please

FOR OBVIOUS reasons, I don't like the subject
of this chapter, but in honesty I felt it had to be included. This is where I so often gave up writing
this book. When I began to relive all the pain, the
fears, the emptiness, and the despair, I'd tell myself I couldn't possibly make you believe that you
could ever get over your grief. I'd go over all the
reasons widows have for being unhappy—being
alone, outcasts, bringing up children without
help. . . .

All the *negative* aspects of our situation would
weigh me down again, and I'd wonder who I
thought I was anyway, Florence Nightingale?
Florence would have known better than to try to
give hope when there was none. I'd get so depressed concentrating on all the negatives and
thinking about how bad widowhood is at first that
I'd forget all the positives and chuck the man-

uscript back in a drawer until another day when I felt *terrific*, and knew I had to tell you that no matter how miserable you feel now, you will eventually feel terrific again too.

No one I talked to would talk freely about this blackest period—one that many people do not go through at all; but we all know of widows and widowers who have nervous breakdowns or commit suicide, good evidence that some people do go through it. Many people admitted to me that they went through a time when they were unable to perform simple tasks, and were afraid they were "going crazy." So I decided to include this chapter, because many people who read this book might be going through a "dark night of the soul" but be afraid to admit it to others. If you have reached this depth of fear and despair, I hope this chapter will encourage you to seek counseling at least from a friend.

If you have a close friend you can talk to openly about your problems, preferably someone who has been through what you are going through, you probably won't need to seek professional help. Few widows go to "shrinks," even though many of them could use professional help. They hesitate to go because of the stigma attached to mental therapy, as well as for financial reasons. I didn't want to go either, but thank God I finally went, in desperation.

The first six months after Bob's death, I felt I was making progress in overcoming my grief, even though I was miserably unhappy most of the time. Things seemed to be going reasonably well that summer. The kids and I went on a vacation with family and had a great time. I'd managed to work almost every day and had handled most of the legal formalities connected with probating the estate. I even found myself accepting positive ideas about being single that I hadn't been able to admit at first, and I began to have hope for a happier tomorrow. Then suddenly things went from better to worse—then to worse yet—and then I hit bottom.

I had lost my closest confidante. Peggy was "going steady" and getting along so well that it made me unhappy with my own adjustment by comparison. I sensed that the world expected me to "shape up," and I expected myself to shape up; but the harder I tried, the harder it seemed to be for me to cope with life without Bob. I'd wake up shaking like a leaf, like a person with palsy. I felt ready to burst. I'd cry all the way to work. When I screamed out in the car one day, "Where are you, God? Help me, I cannot do this alone!" God didn't let on He'd heard me. I felt I was on my own, and by then I knew I couldn't succeed by myself.

Some people lose touch with reality when they are under severe stress. I never did. That was the trouble. Everything was *too* real. I'm convinced that people go crazy on purpose, because reality is so bad that anything else is better; so they escape into a nice, comfortable fantasy-world where everything is beautiful.

From the first, I'd had a horrible "feeling" that

came and went. It was similar to the feeling you get when you are awakened in the night by a strange noise or by the telephone. It was an all-enveloping fear that I associated with the additional horror of not being myself, the feeling that I was someone else. I didn't like this other person—she was sad and gloomy and no fun at all. I think I was afraid I'd turn into that kind of person permanently and would never be my true self again. But I wasn't thinking all that out rationally then, and no one ever suggested this concept to me.

All I knew was that I felt like myself when I didn't have "the feeling," felt horrible when I had the feeling, and was sure I was going stark raving mad. When it left, I lived in fear of its return. I felt I could cope with anything if that feeling would just go away and stay away. Not that I would be *happy* if it didn't come back; but at least life would be bearable. It has been several years since I have experienced "the feeling" (an anxiety attack), but even now I cringe at the thought of it.

The feeling would be gone for whole days at a time, when I would act and feel "like me." But then when I began regressing, the feeling came back oftener, until it was with me most of the time. And along with the feeling came the inability to do simple things—like making a bed or opening an envelope. Things I normally did without thinking began to take unbelievable concentration.

A story I had often told about two college girls I

knew didn't seem funny to me anymore. They were headed back to school with hangovers from a big party the night before and met a man in the airport one of them knew. She introduced her friend to him; and later, when the girls had boarded their plane, one of them moaned, "Gosh, I wished he hadn't kept on asking me all those hard questions, like 'What's your name' and 'Where do you live.' "

It's no laughing matter when you have to think hard to remember your address and phone number. Every morning I dreaded buttering Jan's toast, wondering to myself if I could do it. Many people I later talked to said they also had this problem for varying periods of time. One woman said she wondered if she could comb her hair. Another felt she couldn't drive a car, although she'd driven for years. One felt she couldn't play the piano, although she'd played the organ in her church for years. One girl said the phone would ring and she'd wonder if she could answer it. A professional woman confessed that she had once left a supermarket, in complete confusion, because she couldn't decide which gelatin to buy.

I couldn't understand why no one seemed to notice that I was acting strangely. Of course I was putting up a "normal" front. I didn't let people see that I couldn't eat. I stopped having lunch at the canteen, because I couldn't swallow solids. I drank my meals for months—milkshakes, eggnogs, soup, liquid gelatin. I said all the right things. I sounded rational. I even laughed at the right times. Yet it surprised me that my legs held me up. I kept on doing things I felt I couldn't possibly do, and kept on acting like a normal person so people wouldn't know that I was not!

I had handled sorrow, but I couldn't cope with this phase. It was fear and panic and horror all rolled into one. One day I went to the employees' physician, begging for a tranquilizer. I'd have crawled a mile to get something that might help—drugs, alcohol, anything. Nothing I got helped, however, and by that point I was sure nothing ever would.

I felt it was just a matter of time before I'd have a nervous breakdown. That was when I decided to move to South Dakota, where I had a sister who could take care of the kids when I cracked up. Twenty-four hours a day I told myself, "Hang on, hang on, it's only a few months until school will be out. Count the days, check them off on the calendar. Once you get moved, you can go to the hospital."

I wanted to shout at people, "Can't you see this is not me?" I got the kids and myself up and dressed for school and work every day, dropped them off at school, went to work, picked them up at the sitter's after work, fixed meals, shopped, did the laundry and cleaning—went through all the *motions* of living, but I was barely functioning. My work was less than mediocre, although I'd received an outstanding work award the year before and knew my job inside out.

I knew I was ready to blow up, and I waited and

wondered—not *whether* the explosion would happen, but *when*. I paced the floor at home, waiting for bedtime. I went to bed early, but couldn't sleep, just watched the clock tick off the hours. I felt safe in bed and unpressured, though, knowing there was nothing I had to do until morning. I'd doze, then jerk upright in a cold sweat, shaking all over, *terrified*. I'd dream dreadful dreams. I'd get up hours before I had to leave for work, wondering if I could *get* there, drinking cup after cup of coffee, and trying to act normal so the kids wouldn't notice that I wasn't.

I'd be working at my desk and wonder if I could get up and go to the canteen for lunch. I'd plan it all out and beg, "Please, God, let me get out of my chair . . . go to the elevator . . . push the button . . ." This experience reminded me of the mental patient a nurse-friend of mine had told me about years before. At recreation she told him over and over to throw the baseball to her, but he acted as though he had not heard her and didn't move a muscle. Then he suddenly shouted at himself, "Dammit, George, what in the hell is the matter with you, George? Throw the damn ball to the damn nurse, George!"—and he threw it as he had ordered himself to do. I gave myself orders all day long, and wondered each time whether I'd be able to do as I was told.

I kept papers on my desk that had to be duplicated so that when I felt I *had* to get up and pace, I could take them downstairs to run through the copying machine. Then when I'd get to the empty copying room, I'd hang on to the table while the copies went through the machine, wondering how I'd get back to my desk. When I got back to my desk, I'd make excuses to go see people about billing and receiving problems so I could move around again. I began catching myself making errors. I sent a patient's funds to the wrong hospital by mistake. I sent a $3,000 check to the wrong company and would have had to pay it myself if the company had not paid it back. I knew I was functioning beyond my lowered level of competency, worried about how many mistakes I was making, and went home and dreamt of auditors.

I told my doctor that I was terribly nervous and depressed and asked him if he thought I should go to a psychiatrist. He said my condition was caused by a hormone misbalance because of my hysterectomy. He gave me some estrogen pills and tranquilizers and said I'd be fine. I wasn't fine, but I was doing a good job of fooling the public, thanks to years of training. Don't show your grief. Act well-bred. Remember, thoroughbreds don't cry. You're a Gannon and a Jones—they're tough. Don't tell other people your troubles. Laugh and the world laughs with you; cry and you cry alone. Take your medicine like a man. Stand on your own two feet. God never gives you a cross you can't carry. Other people have gotten through this; so can you.

All along, I doubted that I could get through it, but I felt the least I could do was give it the old college try! I dreaded being the first one in the family to have a nervous breakdown, but kept on making plans for the day I had one. I had a lawyer put everything in my name and my twin sister's, and I gave her power-of-attorney so that she could handle my affairs when the men in the white coats came and got me. She was hundreds of miles away, so I put notes all around the house marked, "In case of emergency . . ." with her name and phone number.

When my two girls and I took that trip to South Dakota to look things over, I wondered for weeks how I'd get packed and to the airport, and what people would think if I suddenly couldn't put one foot in front of the other. During Thanksgiving dinner after we got there, I remember thinking that I had "forgotten" to call Bob to tell him we have arrived safely—then fought back tears because I didn't have to call. It was seven months since he had died, but patterns formed over years are hard to change.

The fear was the worst part of all. Many people have complained to me about their remembered fears. Some said they cowered in their beds, afraid of everything. The most common escape was to go to bed in a darkened room and pray for sleep. Not just as an escape from their grief, but because they became exhausted from the effort of living through each day, worn out with the fear of living, unable to cope with life, and not wanting even to *try* to cope anymore.

On the heels of the inability to cope and along with the fear came despair and death wishes for many of us. I told myself, and have heard others say: "I'd rather be dead." "There's nothing left to live for." "This is worse than death." "Nothing is fun anymore." "I wish I'd be in a car wreck." When I went on that trip to South Dakota, I wanted to walk up to the ticket counter and say, "Three tickets on a plane crash, please." I prayed fervently that it would be God's will to let the plane crash with all three of us on it. It seemed like the perfect solution—but God would not cooperate.

I was "going under" for the last time when I called a psychologist for an appointment. I don't remember what I said when I called, but I practiced for days so I would be dignified about it and not break down and cry. I'd just tell him the truth, matter-of-factly. I needed help. I must have been convincing, because he saw me on his lunch hour—sandwich in hand.

I was then working in the accounting department, but I had previously worked in the mental hygiene clinic of the Veterans Hospital, and what I learned in that clinic about mental health probably saved me from a complete nervous breakdown. When I felt myself losing ground and becoming less able to cope, I recognized the symptoms of severe depression; I knew I needed help and where to go to get it when I finally could bring myself to ask for it.

Someday the social stigma attached to one's receiving treatment for depression and stress will disappear. It will be like going to a doctor or dentist. We'll go when we need help coping with pressures on the job, in our marriages, with our kids, after a loved one dies, when adjusting to new jobs, moving, retiring, and so forth. We'll go *before* we're desperate.

Dr. Brown didn't wave a magic wand and make all the pain and heartache go away that day. Not by a long shot. But he gave me what I needed—*hope that I would get better*, because by then *I* had given up all hope. I also felt better afterward because I had the satisfaction of knowing *I was trying to help myself* get out of the pits.

Counselors and therapists (psychiatrists, psychologists, social workers, etc.) help you help yourself. If you are not talking out your problems with *someone*, and feel yourself going backward steadily instead of going ahead, *go to a counselor*. Select one carefully. Don't go to any counselor, anymore than you would go to any doctor or dentist. And don't let your friends or relatives persuade you that you don't need help *if you think you do*. You know how you feel, they don't. Ask your doctor or the local hospital or Mental Health Association to refer you to someone. In most communities, there are mental health centers subsidized by the government, where treatment can be obtained at minimal cost. The fees vary according to your income.

The whole principle of treatment is to talk out your problems with someone trained to help you work your way through them and able to give you support and encouragement. Treatment takes time, so don't expect instant relief. One of my advantages in treatment was the fact that I could talk openly about my feelings. This ability is very important because, if you won't or can't tell the therapist what is bothering you, it is going to take a longer time for him to help you than if you tell him frankly how you feel.

Therapists care. I have worked with a great many of them, and "I never met a shrink I didn't like." They couldn't stay in the business if they didn't want to help people.

Long-term treatment in cases of stress is seldom necessary. I made thirteen visits over a five-month period. On my first few visits, I was so upset that I had trouble remembering, so I kept notes on what we talked about. I paced the floor during one entire visit, too agitated to sit down. On the first visit, I told Dr. Brown about "the feeling" and about being terrified, I didn't know of what. I also complained of nausea, headaches, and an inability to sleep, eat, or sit still. My symptoms were typical for people under severe stress.

The first advice Dr. Brown gave me was to let myself *experience* the feeling when it came. He told me not to fight it and to think about exactly how it felt so I could explain it to him the next time I came. He said we should let ourselves experience all our emotions, including those of fear and grief, and that once I stopped fighting the feeling I would lose my fear of it and it would no longer have control over me. He also advised me not to "pretend" everything was fine. If people asked how I felt, I was to tell them I felt blue or miserable if that's how I felt.

So I went home and let myself experience the feeling completely, but I was never able to explain it. It wasn't simply a sense of fear and clamminess; it was my whole being enveloped in what I suppose must have been a fear of living, because living at that time was so terrible for me. Allowing myself to think about the pain and horror of it, so that I could put it into words for Dr. Brown, gradually helped me lose my fear of it, however, just as he had said it would.

Treatment permitted me to blow off steam, and gave me ideas about life in general, as well as techniques to help ease my pain. One idea was especially helpful. I kept complaining that I didn't feel "normal." One day the doctor asked me what I meant by "normal." I replied, "Well, *right,* you know. *Like myself.*" Then he said:

"What is 'normal' weather, Jean? Sunshine? Rain? 'Normal' weather is *all kinds of weather*—cold, hot, stormy, balmy, snowy, windy, et cetera. It is normal to have all types of weather. And it is normal for people to experience all kinds of emotions during a lifetime—love, hate, joy, sorrow, anger, bitterness, pain, fear, ecstacy, loneliness, depression, and happiness."

I had never thought about life from that viewpoint. I had interpreted "normal" living as a very small range of emotions, with love being the only "normal" intense one. It was easy for me to see the fallacy in my thinking, and that life actually included experiencing a multitude of emotions. Which is where the saying comes from: "How can you appreciate the heights until you have been to the depths?" We wouldn't even appreciate happiness, or know that *that* was what we were experiencing, if we had no sad experiences to contrast with our happiness.

Dorothy Dix had a tragic life, yet when someone asked her how she had stood it, she said she wouldn't have had it otherwise, because she had *lived* while most people only *existed*. Some people experience only a handful of emotions in a lifetime; she had been "privileged" to have experienced most of them.

Dr. Brown felt that dreams were important and asked me to try to remember mine, so I wrote them down when I'd wake up from one. One kept reoccurring, and it didn't take an analyst to understand it. In my dream I'd awaken in the night and go to turn on the bedroom light, but when I touched the switch the walls of the house crumbled and fell in on me. The night Bob died, I'd gotten up to turn on the light and found that he was already unconscious—and my "house" fell in on me. Other dreams showed us how much fear I had of being alone, of responsibility, and other such fears. Many women have told me they dreamt their husbands came back to life and consequently became terribly worried about how they would pay back the insurance money—showing feelings of guilt and fear. Some women dreamt their husbands had gone off with other women, showing their feelings of rejection and abandonment.

Dr. Brown also suggested that I "say good-bye" to Bob. He felt that subconsciously I was refusing to say good-bye, refusing to "let him go." So he suggested that I have an imaginary conversation with Bob and discuss my plans for the future with him, and then *say good-bye.*

This principle is very important. We widows have to say good-bye before we can move ahead. Our husbands are no longer a part of the world in which we now must live, and the sooner we can make a new life for ourselves without them, the happier we will be. I am not saying we have to stop loving them, or even stop thinking about them, but only that we need to stop living as though they were still alive. A man told me his sister-in-law made every decision on the basis of what she felt her husband would have wanted her to do—*years* after he died. I thought of Bob when I bought a compact car recently. He hated small cars, but he isn't the one who has to drive this one—I am.

My grief progressed into bitterness, which happens to all of us. I was filled with resentment that *this* had happened to *me.* Why to me, and not to others I knew, particularly people older than I? In one session, my psychologist said, "You're bitter, aren't you?" I never admitted it. I thought it was pointless to tell him how I felt. Remember what he'd said about being alone? How could he know what it was like? His wife was at home waiting for him. He *didn't* know what it was like—because he hadn't been there—*but he helped anyway.*

Therapists know we hurt. They know the patterns of grief even though they haven't experienced the pain; just as a male doctor knows how to help a woman who is having a baby, even though he has never had one.

During one particular session, I was crying the blues over the vacuum-cleaner belt's breaking and my having to fix it. In the midst of my complaining, Dr. Brown said, "You poor widow, you, all alone and helpless." He explained that those were the kinds of thoughts I was feeding myself. I was constantly pounding negative ideas into my head, which made it impossible for me to be happy. How could I be happy when I kept telling myself over and over that I was unhappy?

He tried his best to get me to change my self-image as a widow, but he had very little success. It would be years before I changed that destructive widow-image and felt like a worthwhile person. He tried hard enough, God knows. He asked me why I didn't like myself, and told me that the reason I didn't like being alone was that I didn't like myself. There was truth in his diagnosis, but there is more to it than that.

Wives whose husbands travel tell me they can't understand why I would mind being alone, because they don't mind it a bit when their husbands are away on business. They don't seem to understand the difference between being *alone,* and being *lonely*; between being alone *temporari-*

ly, and being alone *permanently*. We can and must learn to enjoy being by ourselves, but we must arrange our lives so that we are frequently with others who care about us and about whom we care—or we will be lonely.

Dr. Brown applied the principle of developing an awareness of the *right now* in a way slightly different from that which I had been using. I had forced myself to concentrate on what I was doing and what people were saying. He told me to be completely aware of *everything* around me—to look closely at, and think about, the shape of a glass, the color of a bird, the formation of the clouds, the pictures on the wall, the types of furniture in a room, the clothes people were wearing, and so forth. Doing so, he said, will take your mind off your grief and teach you to enjoy the beauty of things around you.

I hung on between visits. The weeks were busy enough to keep me rushing around thinking of the "now" much of the time; but the week-ends were more intensely depressing. I dreaded them. The minutes dragged by with nothing to look forward to. I was unhappy most of the time, and impatient with myself for being that way.

Impatience with oneself is among the sadder things about depression. As Daniel Considine observes, "Not to lose patience with ourselves when we feel depressed is a very high virtue." When they are depressed, "people really believe that they have lost faith, hope, love, everything. It is a very great trial."

Depression is experienced most frequently by people who set their goals too high and demand too much of themselves. They become depressed when they fail to meet their own expectations or the expectations of others. Widows most certainly fall into this category. They expect too much of themselves, feeling they should adjust to their grief and numerous problems rapidly; that is what they feel society expects them to do. When they fail to meet their own expectations and the expectations of society, they become deeply depressed.

Dr. Van Coevering, in her doctoral studies of factors that affect widows' sense of self-satisfaction, found that "it takes two years for widows to feel part of any new psychological and emotional environment. . . . One out of every four widows is still emotionally ill in the third year of widowhood, . . . and some widows never come out of the depressed state of grief and grieving." Two major factors are responsible for this failure among widows to overcome their sense of depression. First, women are taught from childhood to be almost totally dependent upon a man financially and emotionally. Second, we are *not* taught how to overcome grief.

Professional treatment, friends who have been there, or widow-support groups can help you change *your* attitudes about being independent, and teach you how to handle your grief appropriately and successfully.

Treatment helped me to see that I was making ridiculous demands of myself. I gradually became less upset as I applied the ideas and techniques that Dr. Brown presented to me. I was still emotionally ill when I moved to South Dakota from West Virginia a year after Bob's death. I was to be plagued with "the feeling" (anxiety attack) off and on for another two years, but treatment enabled me to lose my fear of it. Treatment got me through the worst hours of my grief and despair. It did not make me happy, but it gave me hope, which is the first step toward happiness.

My "plans" to have a nervous breakdown persisted for two more years, but to my irritation there was never a convenient time to have one—a fact that finally forced me to give up the idea entirely!

The ideas presented to me in treatment may be summarized as these:

1. Permit yourself to experience fully such feelings as grief, fear, guilt, and bitterness. Admit you are having these feelings, then ride them out. You will feel better afterward. If you hold them back, they will build up and overwhelm you.

2. Do not tell others you feel fine *if you don't.* Don't go into detail explaining how you feel except to a confidante, but be honest about it.

3. Don't tell yourself you "should" do things. Say to yourself instead, "I *will* do this." Make it your choice, not what you feel someone else thinks you should do.

4. Don't refer to your possessions as "ours" anymore. When you say "my" car, "my" house,

you are accepting your situation and living in the present instead of the past.

5. Think about your dreams. They may help you discover your subconscious attitudes and thereby enable you to face and work through them.

6. Make new friends. Try new activities and hobbies. Join organizations you think you will enjoy.

7. Have an imaginary conversation with your husband in which you talk over your future plans and tell him good-bye so you can move ahead without him.

8. Once you make a decision, do not make it over a dozen times. Think a problem through carefully, decide what is best for you to do, and then do it without regrets.

9. If you think of yourself as an unhappy widow who isn't any fun anymore, you will convince yourself that you are that kind of person. Think of yourself realistically instead, as a person who is handling a severely stressful situation as best you can.

10. Be fully aware of everything and everyone around you. You cannot think of two things at once, so this concentration on your present surroundings will let you forget your grief part of the time.

11. Do not be afraid of being alone. Being alone (part of the time) permits you to get to know and like yourself.

12. "Normal" feelings include all emotions,

just as normal weather includes all types of weather. We grow through our experiences. When we experience many emotions, we live a fuller life than those people who have experienced only a few, and we become stronger persons as a result.

CHAPTER EIGHT

Grieving Time

THE SIXTY-FOUR dollar question every widow asks is, "How long is it going to take to get over it?" Unfortunately, time heals slowly. Most widows I've discussed that question with said it took them approximately two years to adjust.

The one-year mark is extremely depressing for most widows. I attribute this timing to the fact that they feel they are "supposed" to adjust in a year; and if they do not feel great by that time, they become alarmed and discouraged. It actually takes a year to comprehend fully all the aspects of widowhood; consequently, widowed men and women frequently go into deep depression at the end of a year's time. It is usually after this major setback, however, that we begin to make real progress in facing and *enjoying* our new way of life as much as possible.

Very few people make the adjustment rapidly.

I've talked to some women who appeared to be very well adjusted within a year, but many more who took much longer.

There doesn't seem to be any common denominator to determine how long it will take to adjust. For instance, it doesn't seem to make any difference how "religious" one is; many people, however, think that a religious attitude of "accepting God's will" is helpful. It doesn't seem to matter if you have been widowed once before. One man, widowed twice, told me he found it easier to adjust the second time. A woman, also widowed twice, felt it was much *more* difficult for her to adjust the second time when she was much older. Generally speaking, older people appear to accept widowhood more easily because so many of their friends are also widowed, a fact that gives them more "available" companions. Some older women have told me, however, that it was harder for them because they had been used to being married that much longer.

Some people are of the opinion that if a marriage was less than ideal, the widow should be expected to adjust rapidly. This is not the case. Some of the people I've consulted who had the largest problems in their marriages also had the hardest time adjusting. How many marriages are "ideal" anyway? Not many. I only knew one, and it wasn't mine! Most marriages are "average," with problems galore.

One man's wife was a shrew if I ever saw one; but it was pathetic to see how much he missed her when she died. He was old, and her death turned his life upside down. He was used to her griping, but he wasn't used to eating alone.

The widow of a man who cheated on her all the time almost had a nervous breakdown when he died. She loved the louse.

People who might be expected to have a very difficult time adjusting, sometimes do adjust rapidly. For instance, a woman who lost her husband and had to go to work to support her three small children said she was so busy working and trying to figure out how to make her salary stretch to keep food on the table and a roof over their heads that she didn't have time to grieve! Another woman in almost these same circumstances had a nervous breakdown.

A reporter once interviewed a retired widower who had been a popular athlete. The reporter wrote that the man repeatedly referred to the fact that his wife had died five years ago, and drew the obvious conclusion: he still missed her terribly.

A woman widowed nine years told a man newly widowed, "You never get over it." She later apologized, saying, "I shouldn't have said that. You get used to it in time, but you never get over being sorry it happened, and you never forget." (These two married each other a year later.)

The mother of two children said she finally began to adjust after eight months when an aunt told her, "I know it's hard, but each day you spend in grief is one you are giving away, and life is too precious to waste."

Shortly after Jacqueline Kennedy moved out of the White House, she told a friend to come over because she had "nothing but time" left. A year later, reporters said she talked of JFK "at great length" when people came to visit; eventually it was reported that it took her three years to adjust, under the most supportive of circumstances.

When asked "How long does it take to get over it?" one woman said, "You can't tell, but some morning you'll wake up and everything will be all right again." Another said, "If you enjoyed life before, you will again; if you didn't before, you won't now." Both are true statements, but do not tell you *how long* it will take for you!

How rapidly or how slowly someone else got over the grief, however, *does not have anything whatever to do with your adjustment.* It doesn't make any difference how long it took a friend, or Elizabeth Taylor, or Old King Cole to adjust. *Your* adjustment depends entirely on your own set of problems—*problems only you know about.*

I believe I adjusted when I stopped waiting. Waiting for the pain to stop? Waiting to be rescued by a knight in shining armor? Waiting to wake up and have everything be all right again? It took me three and a half years to stop waiting and start enjoying life as a widow. At that, I feel lucky not to have "wasted" more of my life. One woman said it took her nine years to adjust. I am not apologizing for the years she and I lost. We did the best we could. Who can do more?

CHAPTER NINE

Rings and Things

I T W A S interesting for me to find out that we all have hang-ups as a result of our negative attitudes, and that many of them are similar. The best piece of advice I was given was: "If you can't change a situation, change your attitude about it." Unfortunately, changing our attitude about something is not easy for any of us.

"Widow" is not a nice word

Many words "hit us wrong." When the children were small, we told them that some words were "nice" and others were not. *Widow* is not a nice word; at least, all widows seem to hate the word. It made a world of difference to me when my lawyer's secretary said, "This is Mrs. Jones," compared to another introduction I was given at the place where my husband worked: "This is Bob Jones' widow."

We gradually get used to the word, but at first the label makes us cringe. Some women have told me that as soon as they began calling themselves widows, the word didn't sting as much. Few of us could do that for a long time, and we resented it when others used it of us; but the more often you are able to say the word yourself, the faster it will stop causing you pain. Kidding about it, when you can, works wonders.

A beautician-friend of mine told me that one of her customers who had been widowed for several years referred to a friend as "not married either." The woman then paused and added, "I should say she's a 'widow' too, but I hate the word!" She was still answering the "ouch" bell.

Most of our sources of mental or emotional difficulties as widows don't make much sense, but the word *widow* is bound to hurt us at first, because it carries with it all the pain, fear, loneliness, anger, and frustration we associate with our despised new life. You will hate the word *widow* until you accept yourself as one.

Address my mail to Mrs. Robert Jones

This topic is a sore spot for all widows. It upset every new widow I talked to to get mail addressed to her by her first or given name. At least once a year, Ann Landers has a letter in her column from a widow complaining about it. The etiquette books state very plainly: "It is not proper to address a note or social letter to a married woman, *even if she is a widow*, by her given name. A widow always keeps her husband's name." A widow generally uses her husband's name because it is socially correct to do so.

It made Peggy and me depressed—and angry—every time we got a letter addressed to us improperly. Seeing "Mrs. Jean Jones" on the envelope was enough to ruin my day. A relative of one widow told her she *purposely* addressed her letters that way because she was afraid it would make her feel worse to see her husband's name on the envelope—another example of people who are *trying* to help us, who really *care* about us, but who are doing exactly the *wrong thing* without knowing it.

I sometimes use some classy stationary engraved "Mrs. Robert Burke Jones," but I have done a complete about-face concerning my own name. "Jean Jones" is *me*, a widow. I am a person in my own right now, and I like my name. I'm not ashamed of it! I *prefer* it with the "Mrs." attached, which shows I still have a minor hang-up, but I don't need to lean on the "Robert" anymore.

You may prefer *your* given name one of these days. Many young married women have a hang-up in the opposite direction about names and don't even change theirs when they get married. I read an article by an irate young wife whose husband (surname "Smith") objected to her getting her mail directed to "Mrs. Mary Smith" instead of to "Mrs. Harold Smith." She said her mother had named her *Mary*, not *Harold*, and she felt her identity was being threatened when people addressed her by her husband's name. So it's all in the attitude!

Wedding rings are beautiful

I have never seen a widower wear a wedding ring; but most widows continue to wear their wedding rings. In case you are wondering, the etiquette books say: "Widows may leave their rings on, and most women prefer to, especially if they have children, right up until they should remarry. If she becomes engaged, a widow either removes her first wedding and engagement rings or else transfers them to the fourth finger of her right hand. But when her second engagement ring is given her, she puts aside the first and if her second marriage is to take place soon, she removes her wedding ring as well."

Peggy and I felt it was a sign of progress to remove our rings: a sign we were accepting our widow role and were ready to date, should anyone ask us! We had a tough time leaving them off, however. I felt my rings were a link to Bob. I still *felt* married to him, so I went back to wearing my rings. I not only wore my wedding ring on my left hand (engraved *All my love and all my life, Bob*), but I also wore *his* wedding ring on the other hand! But now again, I hardly ever wear those rings anymore. Recently, during a traumatic experience I had to handle alone, I purposely put them on again for moral support.

A woman I worked with began dating immediately after her husband died, and took her wedding rings off immediately—which showed she had the strength and the wisdom to go ahead, instead of wasting her time living in the past. Most women continue to wear their wedding rings because the rings are beautiful. Perhaps they are also a sign—to us and to others—that somebody "up there" loves us. One woman I know who was married and widowed twice wears a set of rings on each hand. Again: do what you prefer.

Normal anger and regrets

Another stage that we commonly go through is a period when we are angry at our husbands for having died, feeling as though they had deserted us on purpose. Peggy and I talked about what a dirty trick it was for our husbands to "cop out" on us. We laughed when we said it, but underneath we were angry about it. We wives seem to interpret "until death do us part" to mean until *we* die, not our husbands; and we resent it when they fail to keep the agreement.

I saw a comic strip not long ago that I wish Peggy and I could have shared back then. It showed a woman in bed, supposedly talking to her dead husband, who was shown in a little wispy cloud over her bed. When she asked him what she should do about the plumbing and their teenagers, he answered, "But *dear*, have you forgotten? I've passed on," and poofed out of the cloud. The woman sighed, looked out at the reader, and complained, "George always did take the easy way out!" Peggy would have *loved* it!

There's a song that goes, "You picked a fine time to leave me, Lucille, with four hungry children and a crop in the field." No matter *when* our husbands die, we complain bitterly, "You picked a fine time to leave me."

We each also direct our anger at others, feeling they are responsible for our husband's death. I felt that Bob's job had killed him. One woman said she blamed the doctor for not having saved her husband's life. One man blamed the ambulance driver for not getting his wife to the hospital in time to save her life. We blame the boy who didn't get there to shovel the walk, or the nurse who didn't check often enough. We want to blame somebody, so we strike out at any fall guy we can find, including the dead. Those who had lost their spouses in accidents were the most angry. In time, however, we each come to accept the fact that it was clearly the time for our husband to die, even though we do not understand why.

You will probably blame yourself, too, for your husband's death. You think: if you had done this or that, it would not have happened. If you had made him take it easier, if you had insisted that he go to the doctor, if you hadn't asked him to shovel the walk, he'd still be alive. We have so many regrets, and regrets are foolish; but they are a stage of grief that *we all go through.*

We think of millions of things we wish we had done, and millions of others we wish we *hadn't* done. We ask ourselves why we didn't sit down and watch TV with our spouses more often, why we didn't fix their favorite meals more often, and why we argued over anything.

It is impossible to live with anyone without hurting that person at times. Every couple has arguments over finances, over buying a new sofa or a new car, over the kids and vacations. It's foolish to make yourself miserable thinking back over the things you think you did "wrong." Your husband did plenty of "wrong" things too, remember.

A woman who had nursed her husband for years before he died nevertheless felt she should have been more compassionate. Another felt guilty because she had griped about his watching ball games on TV all the time. Regrets are a waste of time. I know, because I wasted a lot of time on them.

What most widows regret the most is not having told their husband how much they loved them more frequently. I'm sure our deceased loved ones know—now—all the things we wish we had said, and all the things we are sorry we did say. And even if you are not fortunate enough to believe that, what difference does it make now? You can't go back and live your life over. So try not to make things tougher for yourself by harboring useless regrets.

I CAN do it myself

A source of much frustration and self-pity among us widows is having to do a man's work around the house. I think the biggest headache we have in common is keeping a car going. You will even hate to get gas if your husband used to keep the gas tank filled for you; and having to think about grease jobs, oil changes, antifreeze, and car washes will depress you.

It took me almost a year, but I finally made a friend of my car. Now I feel smug when I recognize words like "carburetor," "transmission," and "fuel pump." My daughter Leigh Ann loves to work on cars. She's proud of the fact that she knows more about engines and mechanics than most of her boy friends do. The last time I took my car into the repair shop, there were five men in the shop. The car was making a funny noise. All five of the men came over and stuck their heads under the hood to listen to its heartbeat. Each one made a different diagnosis, trying to out-guess the mechanic. It dawned on me then that car repair is a fun thing that we women have been missing out on.

Don't be afraid of your car! Take it to a reliable service station regularly and ask a good, honest mechanic to tell you what needs to be done. Ask around; people will tell you in a hurry who is reliable. Mechanics are nice to women. They like us better than the know-it-all men who come in and try to tell them their business. Also, *read the Operator's Manual in your glove compartment.* You'll be amazed at the things you'll learn!

Hammers aren't *all* bad, anymore than cars are. Doing minor repair jobs around the house isn't as hard as you think. It's actually no more trouble for me to do some jobs myself, now that I've learned how, than it was talking Bob into doing them and running back and forth handing him tools! He had me fooled all those years, into thinking some jobs were hard to do—but aren't.

The first household "repair" I had to do alone after Bob died was change the belt on the vacuum cleaner. I ended up crying. Now I can pound nails in straight (about fifty percent of the time), hang curtain rods, thaw out frozen water pipes, start the power mower and snowblower, use an electric drill, and tackle small repair jobs with some confidence.

The proper tools are all-important. Your husband probably had the tools you will need in the garage or basement; so all you have to do is learn how to use them. Get someone to show you how. Ask your son or brother-in-law; they'll be more than happy to show you. Ask a kid to show you how to operate the do-it-yourself car wash. Take a course at your local trade or high school. Friends will be glad to tell you what tools you will need to paint or wallpaper, and show you how.

You will probaby feel licked before you even *try* to hit a nail on the head the first time, but practice makes perfect. Try an easy job first. Ease into the bigger ones. You'll find you are better at some things than at others, but you won't know what you can do until you have tried. I know women who can change tires, replace faucet washers, stop toilets from running, and jump cables (or something) to start cars.

If you can afford it and can find a good handyman who will do small repair jobs, you are lucky. *Lucky if you have the money, and lucky if you can find a handyman who will do them!* Which is why most of us start trying to do things ourselves, and end up pretty good at it and even enjoying it. One widow I know, in her fifties, took a carpentry course at her local trade school and built a stairway and finished off her attic all by herself! When we all get *that* great, it's really going to be hard to be humble!

To move or not to move

Many widows and widowers are faced with the problem of whether or not to move from their homes after their spouse dies. The reasons are numerous. The house is too big. It costs too much to keep up. It's too much work for one person. They are afraid to live alone. They feel there are too many memories and think it will help if they move. Sometimes they are running away from their grief, hoping to leave it behind.

Don't do anything in a hurry. A year is a good yardstick in this case. Sometimes, however, you cannot postpone moving. A farmer's wife wisely moved into an apartment in town and rented her farm in the fall, right after her husband died. *She did not burn her bridges behind her, however, by selling the farm.* That winter she found out she didn't like apartment living but got used to living alone and coping with problems; so she moved back to the farm the following fall. She intends to sell her farm eventually and buy a small house in town with a little yard for her flowers, but she's taking her time about doing it.

One woman who was afraid to live alone but who valued her privacy and yard sold her home and bought a duplex. She is no longer afraid because she is not living in a house all by herself, and she has the privacy and yard she enjoys.

Many widows sell their homes and move into apartments. The interest on the money they get for their houses is generally more than the cost of renting an apartment, and they feel safer in an apartment and do not have the responsibilities connected with keeping a house in repair. Apartments are also less lonesome and more convenient for singles, as there are people with whom to socialize without even having to go out of the building. Some widows sell large houses and buy smaller ones. Others remain where they are.

Moving to another area is usually disastrous *if done too soon*. Most people who have done so have told me they regretted it. They found they had tried to run away from their grief, and actually took it with them and *added* to their problems by having to adjust to a strange place full of strangers.

If, however, after a year or so you feel you might be happier elsewhere, do not be afraid to move. You can always move back if you don't like the new residence. One widow of seven years recently retired from her job, sold her home, and moved to a city several hundred miles away, *and is glad she did.* There is more for a single woman to do in a city, and she has a number of friends there, some of whom live in the same apartment building. (It is a sign of her terrific adjustment that although she gets along beautifully with her only daughter, she did *not* move even to the part of the country where her daughter lives.)

An older widow I met on a plane one winter said she moved to Phoenix five years after her husband died *and wished she had moved sooner.* She was enjoying her life more and meeting more new people in Phoenix than she had "at home."

I waited a year to move, and found that moving helped me to "start over." But it doesn't work that way for everyone.

Someone said there is only one thing harder than living *with* someone, and that is *living alone.* You will be lonely at first, but give it careful thought before you have anyone move in with you. Later you are apt to prefer living alone, and hard feelings could result if you ask your friend or relative to move out. There are exceptions to this advice, of course. Widowers frequently move in with a daughter, sister, or aunt; and this decision seems to work out well for them. A widower with young children often needs the help of a live-in relative or friend. A widowed friend of mine has lived with her widowed mother-in-law for years, and the arrangement has worked out very well. Sometimes sisters who are both widows live together, and this arrangement also seems to work out fine. One widow's niece moved in to help her with the children and to babysit when she went out.

There is no question that it would save money to have a friend or relative move in to share expenses; but most widows apparently treasure their privacy, because the majority of us prefer to live alone unless we remarry.

Women en masse drive me bats

By far the biggest hang-up of all for widows is the "I-hate-women" syndrome. Long ago widows were included in social affairs along with everyone else, but this is no longer the case. Single men are sometimes invited to parties alone, but single women seldom are invited to couple affairs without an escort. The younger people are gradually changing this situation, but that does not help the widow over forty, who is almost forced by society to spend most of her time with women. The fact that there are many more single women than single men is also a factor.

This situation is so threatening at first that a widow may hate to be seen with another woman, particularly if that woman is another widow. Society's suspicious attitude about homosexuals has much to do with our fear of being seen with women, especially being seen regularly with one particular friend. You probably did not worry about that before you were widowed, however, *so why worry about it now?* Let people think what they like. *That's their problem, not yours!*

I wish all widows had men friends as well as

women friends with whom to go places. Because of our normal attraction to the opposite sex, an all-women environment may seem abnormal. For this reason, we often envy married women.

If we compare our lives to those of married women, however, we must compare them to *all* married women—the happily married women, who lead enviable lives, and the unhappy married women, who often live lives of "married loneliness." True, our lives are not as happy as those in the first group, but *if you are making any happiness happen at all,* you are much happier than those in the second group.

If you do not have a man to escort you places, *try to change your attitude about going places with women.* We so hate the thought of an all-women world at first that we forget that we spent a great deal of time with other women *by choice* before we were widowed—because we have more in common with women than with men, and because we enjoy their company.

I hope your life includes seeing men at work as well as socially. I will talk about arranging your life so that you do have that kind of relationship, in a later chapter, for it is important. But at the same time, you should not shy away from associating with women.

A hesitation to be seen with other women after we are widowed (as was true with Peggy and me) is often a sign of our own denial to ourselves that we are widows. Subconsciously we feel a repugnance at being *one of them* and want other people to forget that we are. For any or all of these reasons, the I-hate-women feeling is painful and frustrating and difficult to overcome.

Remember that *married or single,* you and I are as important to the community as anyone else is. Widows are often more involved than others in community projects. Yet the stigma you yourself attach to widowhood may be so strong that you may answer the "inferior" bell all your life, alone or with women friends, in social situations. *If you let yourself feel inferior to married people* in these situations, *you are adopting the very attitude that you resent society's having toward you!* There is no reason why you cannot enjoy a cocktail party, for example, as much now with a woman friend as you did before with your husband *if you have the proper attitude about yourself and about women in general.*

My idea of women's relationships has gotten into a proper perspective again. *It is the same as it was before I was widowed.* My closest friends have always been women. I like any man or woman who is interesting and good company. Merely because there aren't enough men around is no reason for me to stop enjoying my women friends just as much as I ever did. I went on two fantastic vacations with four other women, and had as much fun as—if not more fun than—I had had on any vacation I ever took with Bob, other than our honeymoon! Which proves again: it's all in our attitude, this time, about women.

Some widows have complained to me that

many of their married women friends "dropped" them socially after they were widowed. This is often the case because of our couple-oriented society, but sometimes the shoe is on the other foot. We frequently avoid being with our married friends because it hurts to hear them talk about their husbands and the "normal" life we have lost. At first I found myself categorizing every woman I saw into one of two groups: the "haves" and the "have nots"—those who had husbands or wives, and those who had not. This classification seemed all-important and regulated my friendships for a long time without my recognizing the fact.

Some widows say they felt that married women *did not want them around for fear their husbands might become interested in them.* This must be true, because I've heard it so often. I say "must be," however, because I do not know it to be true from my own personal experience. I have never been a "femme fatale" and have never felt that any wife considered me a threat to her marriage. I might add that nobody's husband has ever shown a romantic interest in me—which, perhaps naïvely, I consider a compliment. The predatory female, *married or single,* justifiably causes wives concern, and I can understand why she is avoided. I do not think there is in that possibility a sufficient justification for ostracizing widows from couple functions, for *not all widows are interested in someone else's husband.*

Some wives seem to fear widows for another reason. They seem to look upon being a widow as a contagious disease and think they might be tempting fate if they associated with us. This attitude is tied in with a fear of death, and with the fact that they do not want to think that their husbands could and, according to statistics, probably will die and leave *them* widows.

Other wives envy us. There's no doubt about it. They envy us our independence. A woman I know was widowed very young and raised her small children the hard way—clerking in a store. An unenviable situation, you would think; however, a married woman commented enviously, "She's always had her own way about things." (It is interesting that this widow had many chances to remarry but did not.) Most women over forty were brought up with the idea that the man is the "head of the house" and makes all the big decisions on how the couple's money is spent. Some wives even have to ask permission to buy a new dress and are told how much they can pay for it, if they are given permission! It is no wonder these women envy us our financial and social independence.

Widows are a minority group, and as such we feel *different*. I felt uncomfortably different coming home from a bridge club meeting one evening three years after I was widowed. I drove three married women home, and each one made a comment about her husband's "waiting up" for her. When we pulled up to one house, the woman's husband could in fact be seen in the living room, "waiting up" for his wife. I deposited my passengers at their doors and went home to shed some tears before I went to sleep, feeling lonely and bitter.

Recently I learned how far I'd come when I went out for coffee with a group of married women one night after a church meeting. One woman said she'd better hurry home, because it irritated her husband if she stayed out too late. Each of the others made similar comments about how their husbands felt about their being out without them. None of the husbands liked it—not even for a church meeting. This time I thought to myself, "I don't have to worry about what anyone else will say about my being out as late as I want." While I wished Bob *were* home waiting for me, it didn't hurt anymore that he was not. The house no longer seemed empty without him. I was even used to sleeping alone in "my" big double bed. I had adjusted so well that until that minute I hadn't been aware that I was the only single woman in the group. I no longer felt uneasy in that situation, or envious when wives talked about their husbands. I was no longer categorizing my friends as "married" or "single." They were once again *just friends*. It was a good feeling.

Widows all agree that our couple-oriented society often makes them feel uncomfortable when they are out together. Being a widow is a decided disadvantage socially today. Look around, however, and you will see many husbands and wives out together who obviously are not having as much fun as you and your women friends have together. After dating a nice guy, you probably will still have to admit that you didn't have as good a time with him as you sometimes do when you go out with women!

All our lives, as girls, single adults, and mature adults, when we women want to talk confidentially to a friend about something really important, we will almost always talk to another woman: our mother, sister, best girl or woman friend, *because women understand each other,* often better than husbands understand their wives.

Women are wonderful people *even if they are women!* Do you subconsciously think women are "not as good as" men? Do you feel women are *inferior* to men? I don't. Some women are a pain in the neck, but others are terrific—just as men can be one or the other. Except for romantic purposes, there's no difference. *A friend is a friend.*

I do not have a close friend I am with constantly. I no longer wonder about the appropriateness of such an arrangment, however, and would not hesitate to go into such a friendship if I ever met a woman I enjoyed being with that much. For convenience, you may want to do so. It is obvious that these friendships can be rewarding, but I prefer going places and doing things with a number of friends.

I also consider that one of the big *advantages* of my being a widow is the freedom to do what I want to do and go where I want to go—or *not* do something or go someplace—*without consulting anyone else.*

In a close twosome friendship, *with a man or a woman,* you are obligated to consider the other person in your plans, always. Short of marriage, that's too high a price for me to pay for a friend, even though it might make my life more "convenient" and secure.

I like women. I always have and I always will like them, and I intend to keep on enjoying and appreciating *all* my friends—whether they are men or women. How about you?

CHAPTER TEN

I Make Me Sick

YEARS AGO the following gem was passed around at work:

As I sat musing, alone and melancholy,
*   and without a friend,*
There came a voice out of the gloom saying,
"Cheer up, things could be worse."
So I cheered up, and sure enough
*   —things got worse!*

This is what happens to many of us. Just when we start to cheer up, things get worse. And often things get worse because we get sick. And we frequently make ourselves sick.

We make ourselves sick for various reasons—primarily because we lose the will to live. Viktor Frankl, in *Man's Search for Meaning*, wrote of a man in a concentration camp: "His faith in the future and his will to live had become paralyzed, and his body fell victim to illness (typhus) as a result."The prisoners lived with disease all around them constantly, but they resisted infection *until they lost the will to live*. They then lost their resistance to diseases, caught one or another of them, and died of it.

Statistics show that the widowed do the same thing, resulting in death for a large number of them within a year after they have been widowed. They die from many different causes because they have lost the will to live. Don't give up—*life is beautiful*, and will be again for you.

Doctors unanimously agree on the fact that tension and unhappiness cause a multitude of ailments. Tension can cause tightened muscles, which in turn can cause numbness or even temporary paralysis of arms or legs. Migraine headaches are often brought about by tension and apprehension. Ulcers, colitis, skin rash, high blood pressure, and allergies are other common ailments that go hand-in-hand with stress and grief. Almost every person widowed less than two years suffers from at least one of these complaints.

We "make" ourselves sick also because of our need for sympathy. Society says we should not show our grief, so our bodies react in physical disorders brought about by pent-up emotions. Those disorders in turn—ironically—give us a "legitimate" reason for being entitled to sympathy while we are adjusting to the grief we actually needed the sympathy for in the first place!

It is idiotic that we should think we need an

"excuse" behind which to hide our grief, but we do. Society does not consider grief a reason for prolonged unhappiness, but it will permit us to be unhappy about ill health *indefinitely.* So in our fight for survival, we are sometimes forced (sub-consciously, of course) to make ourselves sick in order to get the sympathy society refuses to give us otherwise.

We seek sympathy in other ways. Since we *ob-viously* cannot be happier than the next person, some of us set out to prove to others that we are the unluckiest people in the world and brag "in reverse" in order to obtain much-needed sympa-thy. Some people even develop this pattern as *a way of life,* thereby ruining their chances for hap-piness.

When I was going through this stage, I told my-self I had it worse than anybody and could *prove* it. I had *dozens* of reasons why I had things tougher than anyone else, and I found reinforce-ment for the idea every time anything unpleasant happened to me—from a mosquito bite to a flat tire.

Many of us handle our anger this way. We are "unluckier" than anyone else because we don't have any children at all, or because they are all grown, or because they are all still at home; be-cause we are older than other widows, or because we are younger; because we had to go to work, or because we had to retire. . . . And almost always: because we have one or more mild-to-severe physical complaints.

Perhaps if we knew we were making ourselves sick ahead of time we could prevent getting sick. But I doubt it; and I am not sure it would be all to the good to prevent such sickness even if we could. Being aware of the fact that grief is causing some of our physical complaints should make it possible for us to cope with the discomfort of sickness and disability more appropriately, though, and eventually overcome our "need" to become ill.

The reason I am not sure it would be a good idea to skip the physical ailments, if they are not too severe, is that we need the fringe benefits we get from being sick. It is a better way than most of the other ways in which people handle their anger; it is an acceptable way to solicit much-needed sympathy; and we feel so much better when we get well that life seems lovely compared to being sick.

Those of you who have ever had a migraine headache know how beautiful the world looks when you get over one. After a long seige of illness, when we get well again we are very grateful to be once again *just* a widow, rather than a *sick widow*. At least that's what happened to me, and I have seen the same thing happen to others.

I never had that nervous breakdown I had looked forward to for years, but I made myself sick enough to accomplish the same thing. And when I got sick is when I finally faced up to my total situation and decided to cope. I also learned how to relax for the first time in my life, and came to know and like myself in the process.

It took me a while to make myself good and sick. I moved a year after Bob died, remodeled the old house I'd bought, and went to work part-time as a nurse's aide in a nursing home. Just before I was to quit for the summer when the kids would be home all day, I again began having trouble coping with "life."

I was worried about having company, fixing meals, keeping the kids occupied all summer, and taking them on a vacation. Once again I felt lonely and unhappy. The techniques stopped working for me, and I got tired of trying to make them work; I got tired of pretending to be happy when I was not. My adjustment was shallow because underneath it all I had "hypnotized" myself into believing that I could *never* expect to do more than tolerate my life as a widow. So my body rebelled, and I ended up in the hospital with colitis and then developed that aching back I've already told you about.

I should have become more depressed than ever when my back trouble started, but my aching back had fringe benefits. It gave me an excuse to give up, and it kept me so busy fighting pain that I didn't have time to think of anything else. Fighting pain is like fighting grief—your world revolves around it. I learned to live with pain; and as bad as the pain was, it was not as bad as my depression had been.

It was in this period that I completely accepted myself *exactly as I was,* and began to enjoy my own company. I had to drop almost all social activities, and I stayed home most of the time. Oddly enough, in spite of the pain I awoke to, this is when I stopped waking up depressed and began waking up happy—because I stopped expecting *too much* of myself. I learned how to loaf and enjoy it, because I couldn't do much else for that entire year.

I have never cared for television, but I began to mark off on the TV schedules the programs that sounded good. I was amazed at how much I had been missing on "the boob tube." I knit and did crewel work, and began to read again. I had been too hyperactive to do such things when I was first a widow, because I hadn't been able to concentrate. Now I began reading some of the books I'd wanted to read for years but hadn't had the time for. I also became interested in music again, and listened to recorded music almost constantly. All of which helped me to forget the pain part of the time, and I found myself racking up units of happiness in spite of my self-pity and fear of the future.

My back condition gradually made me totally dependent on others, a fact that I objected to consciously but that probably relieved me subconsciously. My sister drove me to specialists hundreds of miles away for examinations and tests to find out what was causing the trouble. When I went to Michigan to see the neurosurgeon who finally made the diagnosis and operated, I spent six weeks with my twin sister while my sister Nellie took care of my kids back home.

That was the turning-point, when I "got it all together." Maybe that was when I started trusting God. Whatever the reasons, my ruptured back was lucky for me. It put me in what was, at that time, an almost ideal situation. I dreaded my responsibilities and felt alone and unloved. For those weeks away from home, except for the pain, I had everything going my way. I had no responsibilites of any kind. My family had taken them all away from me. I was no longer alone and unloved—I had family all around me, clucking over me. My kids were being taken care of, as well as the house, the yard, and my business affairs—and I basked in my carefreeness for a while, *but not for long.* Before I went into the hospital, I knew that even if the operation was not successful and I had to hire a woman to take care of the three of us, I was going to be happy to go home and live a widow's life.

I left for home the day the doctor said I could—in almost as much pain as when I came, with nothing guaranteed and not a lot of hope. Nothing had changed *except me!* I knew I preferred my own little castle with my kids and all the responsibilities that went with my life, to being dependent on others. I was no longer suspended in space. I no longer felt unloved. I knew I could cope—with the help of God and my friends and relatives.

I had thoroughly appreciated being loved and cared for, but I had missed all the things I hadn't been appreciating since Bob had died. The kids came first, but they headed a long list—from family and friends to the whole town and our house and the Dakota plains! I cried the day before I came home just thinking about the sun coming through my kitchen windows in the morning.

Perhaps while I was gone I decided the kids were a worthwhile "purpose" for living, and in that I fulfilled Frankl's assertion: "He who has a why to live for can bear with almost any how." I'll never know what happened for sure, but I believe I would have felt the same way if my children had been grown and I had come home to an empty house. Whatever the reason, I finally saw clearly that *no matter what the circumstances*, life is precious and beautiful.

My life was never the same after I got back home. I never slid backward again. I didn't have to struggle to find happiness anymore. I had problems, but I had fun too. *I was living.* I still hated being a widow. I still felt that widows had it tougher than just about anybody, but I was appreciating what I did have, and was no longer thinking constantly of what I had lost.

I remained a semi-invalid for another year after my operation, but I did what I could and didn't feel guilty about what I couldn't do. I took depression when it came, and thanked God for the days I wasn't depressed. I took the pain the same way. *Nothing had changed except my attitude.* Six months later, three and a half years after Bob died, I felt I had completely adjusted to life as a widow.

I have seen many widows let their tension and unhappiness give them ulcers, high blood pressure, and heart attacks. One woman developed an allergy, similar to sinus, that reoccurred when she became depressed. Another developed a temporary paralysis of one arm. Countless widows developed ulcers and high blood pressure. When these women got well again, however, they made a happier adjustment. They took up a better overall perspective on things while they were sick, and changed their values—the old story of not appreciating what we have until it is taken away.

When we get sick, we look around and envy the people who are well, and in our eagerness to regain our health we are able to lose our absorption with our grief, so that when we are well again we can appreciate our way of life *in spite of its disadvantages.*

I am *not* suggesting that you develop an ulcer or have a heart attack so that you will adjust faster! I am just telling you that I saw poor health open people's eyes, including mine. Illness taught us to appreciate what we had left; and possibly, if we had worked harder at trying to make some happiness happen *before* we got sick, we might not have gotten sick at all.

CHAPTER ELEVEN

Color Me Green

I HATE this stage, when we are filled with bitterness, resentment, envy, and self-pity. It is the final stage, but the hardest one to get through; the stage where some widows are understandably stuck for life, because they have so much to be bitter and envious about.

Dr. Brown told me there was a lot of anger in me, and there was. There is in most of us. Life has handed us a rotten deal, and we ask ourselves, "Why me, and not someone else?" We think life should be fair—in spite of all the evidence to the contrary. Life is *not* fair, and never has been.

The reason I detest this stage so much is that, after life deals us a low blow, we hurt ourselves even more by our anger and resentment, making a painful situation worse. A divorced woman said, "Bitterness does nothing except poison the person who harbors it. You should accept your lot, get along any way you can, and take things as they come." She had learned about bitterness the way most of us learn—the hard way.

Our bitterness usually begins when we notice that other people do not appreciate the magnitude of our loss. We feel that the earth should stop turning because our husband died, and we become bitter when it doesn't! One woman said she was "madder than hell" at the trees for starting to bud the week her husband died. She said she felt like shouting at them, "How *dare* you? Don't you know that he's dead?"

It's a pity we can't all be widows of famous men, because that is the ideal grief situation. The world *does* stop and give tribute to great men when they die, *and also permits the widows of great men to grieve.* This is not the case for the wives of ordinary men, however. Our husbands left no outstanding footsteps in the sands of time; they were not great in anyone's eyes but our own; but we miss them just as much as great men are missed by their wives, and we should be permitted to grieve appropriately for them.

The widows of famous men were the first targets of my envy. I even envied them their right to wear black. Can't you imagine how people would react if one of us "little" people had the audacity to wear black? We would be labeled eccentric sympathy-seekers.

The widow of a well-known man is able to talk out her grief. People are interested in every little anecdote she can remember about her husband

and their life together for the newspaper articles, books, TV shows, and perhaps even movies that probably will be based on the life of her husband. Her presence is prized at social functions.

Not so for Mrs. Average Widow. She is denied the enviable privilege of talking about her husband for more than a few short weeks, if for that long; and she is dropped socially. Frustration results, and bitterness seeps in.

In the past, people understood the need for mourning, and the dangers of repressing grief. Ancient cultures gave the bereaved the opportunity to express their emotions. For instance, the Jews, when visiting the family after the death of a member, centered all conversation on the deceased for thirty days, which gave the mourners an opportunity to talk out their grief.

Our culture has somehow attached a feeling of shame to any show of emotion. Sophistication does not include tears or undignified emotional "scenes" at funerals. We are therefore forced to repress our grief, and such repression ultimately results in mental and physical illness—*and bitterness.*

Our culture not only does not permit us to grieve; other people in our society are insensitive to our pain (denying death, and the fact that it could happen to them). This insensitivity, apparent in attitudes toward the widow and their painful social exclusion, is one of the major reasons why life is so frustrating for us.

Through no fault of their own, widows usually

find themselves dropped socially. Barbara Walters, in her book *How to Talk to Practically Anybody about Practically Anything* (1970), mentions a woman who had been widowed for years "but was not dropped socially like so many widows." Like almost *all* widows, except widows of famous men. Being ostracized socially is one of the hardest things you will have to accept, and your resentment about it, while justifiable, can grow out of proportion and totally consume you *if you let it.*

For your own sake, overcome your bitterness. To be hurt is unavoidable, but to let that hurt fester until it becomes an open sore is to do yourself more harm than anything or anybody else can possibly do to you. The main thing to remember is that people do not understand what you are going through. Remember that in all likelihood, you were once probably as inconsiderate of widows as others now are of you.

Shortly after Bob died, I asked a co-worker who had been widowed years before why she had never told me how bad it was. She said, "Because you wouldn't have believed me. You wouldn't have understood. Other people don't know what it's like until it happens to them." This is true of any situation. We don't know—and usually don't care much—how bad it is for people who have strokes and become invalids overnight, for instance. Human nature being what it is, we don't know—or care much—about the problems of the elderly *until we are among the elderly.*

Envy and jealousy go hand-in-hand with bitterness, are also *normal*, but destructive. Seeing happily married couples enjoying life is difficult for you because you are missing that way of life, and your husband, so desperately. Envious and bitter feelings are not admirable, but they *are* human, particularly when the majority of people around you have what you do not. If you have what the other fellow has, what is there to be jealous about? It's the same as being good when you haven't been tempted to be bad. So don't feel guilty about your envy and bitterness. Admit to yourself that you have these feelings when you experience them, but don't let them become habit-forming. Try to overcome them. Crying often relieves some of the frustration and takes some of the pain of envy and bitterness away.

Some people fight a losing battle with envy and bitterness, *and become their own worst enemies.* Don't be one of those people, but don't expect yourself never to have such feelings either. One older woman told me (truthfully, I'm sure), "I never let myself indulge in self-pity." I didn't tell her that I indulged in it all the time! She'd never have understood that I *tried* not to, but I succeeded only part of the time. God knows we have plenty of reason to feel sorry for ourselves, and I'm sure *He* understands—even though that woman could not.

One day I went to a party with a group of women, one of whom had gone on a fantastic trip with her husband. On our way home from the party, another widow in the car said, "I know I shouldn't, but I really envy Sallie the trips and fun she has with her husband." *Naturally* we envy our married friends. It's not that we don't want them to enjoy life, it's just that we wish our husbands were still here to do things with us. When women talk about going places with their husbands, we wouldn't be human if we didn't feel twinges of envy.

It is also human to wish that others were more considerate of our feelings. It's true, they should be, but they often are not. I wonder how much we used to hurt widows by comments about our husbands before we were widowed, comments that increased our widow friends' feelings of loneliness and depression? Do we weigh our words about our physical abilities when we are in the presence of cripples? People don't hurt us intentionally, anymore than we hurt others intentionally. No one is handled with kid gloves. Everyone has to develop a tough skin. Blow off steam about how the world treats you to that friend who's been there. She'll understand, and sharing your frustrations will help you both accept the fact that *you have to take the world as it is.* You can't change the world, but you can try to work a change in your own attitude, which will lesson your frustration. Later, after you have worked through your grief, you will be able to turn your resentment into compassion for others around you and channel it into rewarding activities.

When people make remarks that annoy you,

don't "tell them off." They are probably completely unaware that they have said something annoy-
ing. So save your breath *and your friend.* Friends
are hard to come by.

Don't drop a friend because she doesn't "understand." When she insinuates that you should be
adjusting better, remind yourself that she doesn't
know what she is talking about, and don't answer
the "angry" bell.

I get all hot under the collar when people speak
as if they expect widows to adjust rapidly. A cus-
tomer told a widow friend of mine that her grandmother was sleeping all day (withdrawing) a few
months after her grandfather died. The woman
couldn't understand why her grandmother wasn't
adjusting. My friend asked her how she expected
her grandmother to adjust, in a few months, to living alone after living with, and loving, her husband for fifty years.

Another widow friend "socks it to 'em." If
someone says, "I think it's a shame Grace isn't adjusting better," she says softly, "If George had
died two months ago, do you think you would be
used to it now?" She says the person will usually
turn white and admit weakly, "I guess not." Hers
is a good way to get the point home that losing a
husband is not an ordinary, everyday problem to
"overcome."

Many people ask widows how they can help
relatives who have been widowed. They would
like to help them, but they don't know how to go
about it. Most of them do not understand our de-

pression, and quickly become impatient with us.

I often think that the "uncivilized" Indians, who sent widows out of their villages to starve to death, were kinder than our present society is to the widow. A tour-group left our town recently for Vegas, and I saw some raised eyebrows over the fact that two widows were going along with the group, which was otherwise made up of couples. Why the raised eyebrows? The men seemed to object to it more than the women. I wanted to ask them if they had ever thought about how *their wives* would be treated by society if they were to die and leave them widows.

Some people do treat widows like people, though. A married couple I know went to Europe on a tour last year. They became friends with two elderly widowed schoolteachers from the South. The man nicknamed them "Hominy" and "Grits" because of their Southern accent, and both he and his wife felt they were the most enjoyable people in the group. Another couple I know plays penny-ante poker with a group of widows in their neighborhood. They think widows are people just like everybody else. These are two exceptions to society's general attitude toward single women, of course, but that attitude doesn't bother me much anymore, now that *my* attitude about myself and other widows has changed.

I had a completely selfish reason for being nice to people when they hurt me terribly by their remarks and insensitivity to my plight—before I stopped answering the "angry" bell.

I found that when I reacted angrily, I felt miserable. I couldn't live with an angry self-image, so I postponed my anger until I was alone. Try that strategy yourself. Admit you "should be" angry or hurt, but wait until you are alone or with a close friend to get angry. Get good and mad about it then, *if you want to,* but after that, *forget it!* Don't remember it for the rest of your life. After you postpone your anger a few times, you will find that when you think about it later, you will probably decide that whatever it was, wasn't worth being angry about at all.

Before I got proficient at postponing my anger, I developed a neat technique you may wish to try. It uses the same principle as writing a mean letter to someone and then tearing it up. When a woman said to me something like, "My husband never leaves the house without kissing me good-bye," out loud I'd say, "How sweet," but I'd growl to myself, "He's probably overjoyed to get away." If someone said, "Smile and the world smiles with you," I'd answer sweetly, "That's so true," but under my breath I'd snap, "Run that by me again when you're in my shoes, honey!" The only thing you have to remember if you use this technique is not to say the *wrong* lines out loud. You could lose your friends in a big hurry.

I have talked to people so eaten up with bitterness that I could "taste" it. They are *not* enjoyable people to be around, no matter how much they have to be angry about, or how much you pity them. These angry people helped me more than anything else did to rid myself of my own anger—because I could see what it was doing to them, and in that way I became aware of how I was letting my own anger and bitterness make my life more miserable.

I went through a period when I hated the world and everyone in it—my kids, my family, my fellow workers, even the people I saw on television! I hated everyone in this world who was happier than I was. I especially hated everybody who was married. Why did *this* happen to me, and not to them? Why was I the youngest in my family to be widowed? Why did that old couple, walking down the street holding hands, get to grow old together, and not Bob and me? And I'm sure people around me sensed such feeling in me. It's a wonder they didn't avoid me like the plague.

The Monday after Dr. Brown told me to admit my feelings to others, a co-worker came into my office and asked me if I had had a good weekend. I snarled, "No, I did not! Would you believe I'm glad to be back at work?" He looked uncomfortable, picked his chin up off the floor, and left the room—fast. Admitting you feel blue or depressed is one thing, but being obnoxious about it is something else. Venting your anger on those around you will only make them avoid you.

Jess Lair, in *I Ain't Much, Baby—But I'm All I Got,* says being honest about our feelings does not mean getting angry and telling people off. Not only widows, but people in all walks of life make that mistake when they are angry and disappointed with life. These angry people tell you, "I gave that guy a piece of my mind, let me tell you!" Or, "I told her she'd better keep her dog in her own yard or she'd be sorry." Bitterness can change your personality and make you an unpleasant person to be around, if you let it.

Be honest, but don't be hostile. By voicing the fact that you *are* feeling blue today, you alert your friends to the fact that you are not feeling up to par, and relieve yourself of some of the anxiety and tension that build up when you "fake it" and "put on a happy face." If I had answered that man with a sincere, "No, I did not have a good weekend; it's terribly lonesome at home these days," he would have understood and he and his family might have stopped by the following weekend. As it was, I only alienated him. No one likes being around angry people, even if they have a "reason" to be angry.

Many people would like to console us, would like to show they care, but they don't know what to do or what to say. So they avoid us and say nothing. Or they come to see us and say the wrong things. If only they knew that all they have to do is *be* there, and be *patient* with us while we work through our grief.

Sometimes people are inconsiderate and do not include us in their socializing; but other times when friends do ask us over, we are tempted to refuse, and do refuse, to go because we feel uncomfortable and lonelier than ever around couples. So they stop inviting us. We are unpredictable, and they don't understand that the unpredictability is part of our grief.

Bitterness and envy are a part of the grief process—an extremely difficult part for us and for those around us, and terribly hard to overcome. I doubt if we ever overcome them completely. It's easy to read between these lines and see that I have some bitterness left about the way the world treats widows! But it's a far cry from those days when I was so filled up with bitterness and envy that there wasn't any room left for any happiness that came my way.

CHAPTER TWELVE

Mommy, Let's Get Another Daddy

I REMEMBER only one thing the minister said at Bob's funeral: "We mourn with the wife . . . and the children, chosen out of love." I thought to myself numbly, "He means me, *I'm 'the wife,'* and 'the children chosen out of love' are the girls; he means they're adopted." Dark-haired, six-year-old Jan was sitting on my lap, crying softly, not knowing why she was crying. Blonde, ten-year-old Leigh Ann sat at the far end of the mourners' room, as far as she could get from the rest of the family, furious at the world—or God—for doing this to her. Maybe she was still blaming me.

Our children came to us directly from the hospital. Leigh Ann arrived thirteen years after we were married; Jan appeared on the scene four years later. I never quite got over the wonder of having them—not even on days when they were driving me up a wall!

I found them huddled together on the sofa when I got back from the hospital the morning Bob died. Dawn was just breaking. Leigh Ann had her arm around Jan. Both of them looked so little and so frightened. I had barely had time to go into their room a half hour before to tell them I was taking Daddy to the hospital.

On the way home, I had tried to think of a way to break the news to them gently, but when I opened the door I knew there was no "easy way." So I blurted out the unbelievable, "Daddy just died at the hospital." And added, "We're going to miss him terribly." I tried to put my arms around both of them, but Leigh Ann pulled away, her blue eyes blazing angrily. She stood back with her little fists clenched at her sides and shouted at me, "You're *lying*. He is *not* dead. He's not. You're *lying*!" She ran up the stairs. I knew how she felt and called up to her that I had felt like hitting the doctor when I was told, but that it wasn't his fault or anybody else's.

I wanted to ease their pain as I was used to doing when they hurt themselves at play, but no amount of petting would make this pain go away, and I knew it. Touch helps, though, and when Leigh Ann finally came back downstairs, we three sat with our arms around each other, crying, and planned how we'd tell Grandmother. We even laughed when I said I thought we should take a friend of Grandmother's along and Jan said matter-of-factly, "Well then, we'd better go get Abbie." Abbie was my mother-in-law's best friend.

My two daughters have exactly opposite personalities, so naturally they handled their grief in exactly opposite ways. Jan is affectionate and talkative. After Bob died, she demanded more affection than ever, and she let me know just how she felt. One day early in our grief, I mentioned Bob and she said with astute six-year-old logic, "Let's not say 'Bob' or "Daddy,' Mommy. Let's just say 'he,' 'cause that doesn't hurt as much." She cried whenever she felt like it and let me know when she felt sad. Later it became apparent that she found soliciting sympathy so rewarding that she sometimes claimed she was sad when she wasn't!

Two normal characteristics of young children help them in the grief situation. They are very self-centered and have a short attention span. Generally speaking, while they may have frequent periods of grief, these periods do not last long.

A few weeks after her Daddy died, when she accepted the fact that he wasn't ever coming back, Jan came up with the perfect solution to our problem. She rushed into the house one day, all excited, and said, "Let's get *another* Daddy, Mommy. Susan's had *five*!" I told her that was a marvelous idea and that we'd have to start looking around for one—which satisfied her. (To this day, I regret never having met Susan's mother and asked her advice on how to catch *five* husbands!)

Leigh Ann is a quiet, independent person. She

likes affection but never demands it, and has some difficulty accepting it. She shrugged off all efforts of family and friends to console her when her father died, seeming to feel that to accept sympathy or to cry would be a sign of weakness. She even seemed reluctant to let the world know she hurt—like getting a spanking and pretending it didn't hurt.

She showed unusual sensitivity for a ten-year-old, however. On the day Bob died, without saying a word to anyone, she moved his clothes from our double closet to the guest-room closet, so that I wouldn't be hurt by seeing them. After relatives left and we went back to our work-and-school routine, she began bringing me a cup of instant coffee the first thing in the morning, just as Bob had always done. She tried in every way she could to make things easier for Jan and me, even though she was unable to talk about why she was doing these things.

I was determined not to let the girls forget Bob, and assembled a family snapshot album that has served more of a purpose than I had anticipated. That album is a visual diary of our life all those years when we were a "normal' family. It has helped the kids keep their image of Bob as a loving father. They often show the album to friends and point out "our house back in West Virginia." "That's my Dad holding me on his lap" or "me and my folks at my birthday party" or "my Dad with his arm around my Mom." Hardly a substitute for a *live* father, the album was nevertheless visual *proof* that they were loved by a father who once held them and played with them, a father who did not leave them by choice, or because he had stopped loving them.

We are *all* proud of that album. We don't live in the past. We've kept on adding pages of new snapshots of our happy new life together; but all three of us know that we are what we are, and who we are, because of our past association with a loving father and husband, and we have no intention of ever forgetting him or the life we once knew together. In some strange way, that album with its memories of the past, *helps us to be happy in the present.*

It is a hard thing to see your children grieve. Most children adjust fairly rapidly, but their feelings of abandonment at first are intense, and they never feel comfortable about being "different" because they have only one parent. Kids *hate* being different, even if only in the clothes they wear or in the length of their hair. Fortunately most children transfer their love and dependency needs from two parents to the one remaining parent in a relatively short period of time. Some children do take years to adjust, however.

Dr. Haim Ginott, in *Between Parent and Child,* wrote:

A child's greatest fear is of being unloved and abandoned by his parents. Some children feel frightened if their mother is not home when they return from school. . . . A child should not be deprived of his right to grieve and to mourn. Allow children to fully express their fears, fantasies and feelings. The parent may also put into words some of the feelings that a child may find difficult to express. When a child is given the facts simply and honestly, accompanied by an affectionate hug and a loving look, he feels reassured.

Like adult grief, children's grief takes many forms, according to their age and personality. Encourage your children to talk about their feelings of sadness and to show their grief openly, if possible. But *not all children may be able to do so.*

Imagine the fears and insecurity produced in a child when a parent dies! Psychiatrists say the death of a parent may have a delayed effect on children if they are not helped to express their feelings about it. Such children may, for example, become afraid to love another person for fear that person too will be taken from them.

Children often become overly concerned about their mother's health after the death of their father (and vice versa). Teenagers become overly protective of their single parent because of a sense of responsibility for the parent and because of a fear of losing that parent also. Young children are often upset by comments about their mother's "getting old" or "having gray hair." One eight-year-old girl asked her mother to dye her hair. Her father had had gray hair when he died, and her association of gray hair with death produced strong feelings of insecurity in her.

Childrens' biggest problem is the one we all have. We do not know how to handle our grief appropriately. A teenage girl went back to school after the death of her father and told her friends, "My old man kicked the bucket." Her callousness was a defense mechanism. She had no idea how to cope with the situation, and felt that any show of emotion would be considered a sign of weakness by her peers.

College counselors often have to help young people work through the grief of having lost a parent years earlier. The students complain that they have never been able to talk to anyone about their parent's death, not even to "best" friends. Like adults, children have very little opportunity to express their grief and work through it normally. So they bottle it up and consequently are likely to have difficulty in later months or years.

A college girl I knew was having suicidal tendencies, which her therapist felt was a result of her mother's death when the girl was in her mid-teens. A man in his mid-twenties told a teacher he had had in grade school when his mother died that he wasn't able to talk about his grief until years later because his father and his friends would not permit him to do so.

Kids are better able to adjust rapidly *if* they are helped to admit and face the situation and gradually get used to it, rather than encouraged to pretend things are "normal." Be sympathetic but don't sympathize too much. If your child is obviously feeling sad, or crying, you may say,

"You're thinking about Daddy, aren't you?" or put your arm around the child and say, "It hurts, doesn't it? It's really tough. Let's cry a little and we'll feel better. . . . Do you want to go jump rope with Karen?" Suggest that the child help you think of something to do to make you *both* feel better.

I tried to keep myself from crying in front of the girls at first because I thought it added to their grief to see me cry. A friend told me, however, that children often were upset if a parent did *not* cry, thinking that the surviving parent must therefore not have loved the parent who died. Jan proved the truth of this insight when the dam broke for me. I began crying openly after work and she brought me her little pals up on the front porch to peek in the door while she announced proudly, "See, my Mommy is crying about my Daddy." I obligingly kept on weeping while big eyes peered around the door to watch me! It was a relief not to have to "be brave" in front of those little kids. They knew that if you hurt, you cried and felt better!

When Jan complained about our not having a "normal" family, I'd tell her that many children didn't have even *one* parent who loved them; and I made sure she and Leigh Ann knew how much they meant to me. Telling children you love them is important under *any* circumstances, and more important than ever after the death of one parent. We all like to know that we are loved, and touch is one of the best ways to tell someone you love him or her. Open, sincere affection is beautiful, and if children grow up with it, they will be openly affectionate adults.

Child-guidance counselors recommend hugging a child every day and telling her you love her. In helping your children work through their grief, a pat on the arm, the squeeze of a hand, or a hug and kiss can tell them you know how they hurt and that you care. It saves them the frustration of trying to put their feelings into words, if they are unable to express them. Sometimes a sign of affection will help a child "open up" and find the words to talk to you about feelings of fear, pain, and desolation.

Even though given the opportunity, some children, like some adults, cannot talk about their grief, *and do not want to.* Leigh Ann never permitted herself to grieve openly for her father, and I suspect that that was a reason why she had extra problems in her teens, as a result of holding back her tears and letting her anger build up. Like many adults I've talked to, she vented her anger on people and circumstances around her.

At first, when I knew she was thinking about her father, I tried to get her to talk by making leading comments like, "You really miss Daddy, don't you?" But she would either pretend she hadn't heard me or leave the room. She worked through her grief alone, with almost no tears or talking about it—the only way *she* could handle it. Children have to adjust *at their own pace and in their own way, just as adults do.*

Be prepared for your children to be hurt by others. I couldn't believe it when kids taunted the girls about their loss. Jan would tearfully report, "David said, "Ha ha, you don't have a Dad!' " Don't overreact to such situations, because *if you get upset, so will your kids.* Even if you are ready to go out and *behead* the offender, put an arm around your child and say something like, "David is just jealous because you have a new ball."

When your children come in crying that "everybody else has a Daddy," even if your heart is breaking, say as matter-of-factly as possible, "It just seems that way, honey. I know it really hurts. Do you feel like crying a little about it, or do you want a bottle of pop and go back out to play?" (Here again, they'll "work" this angle just to get a bottle of pop if you don't watch out!)

Shortly after Bob died, Leigh Ann came to me with a problem she couldn't handle herself. She told me she thought she had seen her Dad in his car, parked out in front of the house. She also thought she had seen and heard him call to her from outside her bedroom window at night. I told her that I also sometimes felt as if I could almost see Daddy get out of his car, unwind his long legs, and walk into the house in his long, slow strides at five p.m.; but that we were not seeing ghosts. It was just that we were thinking about him so much, we saw him mentally wherever we were used to seeing him—or in our "mind's eye" in the dark—and that we could almost hear his voice because we remembered it so well.

I learned much later that hallucinations are so common among the bereaved that they are considered "normal" by counselors. I have to wonder whether Leigh Ann and I were actually hallucinating, or whether my more "logical" explanation accounts for what we seemed to experience. Children also have upsetting dreams about their deceased parent. When this happens, just listen and sympathize.

Because Leigh Ann seldom expressed any feelings of grief, it made me feel guilty for showing mine. One night, however, I couldn't help it. I woke up about two a.m. and missed Bob so much that I felt I had to be near someone; so I went into Leigh Ann's room and lay down beside her. My crying shook the bed and woke her up. I apologized for awakening her but told her I was so lonesome I couldn't stand being by myself. She put her arms around my neck, and we cried together until we were both exhausted. It certainly helped me, and I think it helped her. When I told her I'd wait for her to go back to sleep and then go back to my bed, she asked *me*, "Are you sure you'll be all right now?" What a child!

There is another, related point that bears mentioning here. Generally speaking, it is not wise to let your children sleep with you at any time, and especially not after a parent dies, unless there aren't enough beds to go around. Once you start such a practice, you or the child may find it difficult to go back to sleeping alone. We have a longstanding rule at our house that if one of us is sick or becomes frightened at night, we go to each other's room to sleep—for moral support. One night, when we were still in West Virginia, we all slept in my bed during a terrible thunderstorm. Another night, not long ago, during a tornado watch, we all shivered together in bed, in a basement bedroom.

Be careful not to make a "big thing" out of what might not be at all traumatic for your child. I got all upset when Jan started school the fall after her father died. Signing her up for school and leaving her that first day were sheer agony for me. I kept thinking about how terrible it was that she did not have a father to come home to, to tell all about that wonderful first day. Well, I don't think Jan ever gave her father a single thought that wonderful day! It was one of the happiest days of her life—Daddy or no Daddy. So don't spoil your children's happiness in any situation by reminding them of the fact that their father isn't around—unless you are pretty sure that they *are* upset about it. This rule holds particularly true at weddings of your children, when *you* probably will feel sad but your son or daughter may not give Dad a thought.

Most of the grief I felt over Jan's first day at school was self-centered. Half the joy of having children is sharing them with the other parent. No one appreciates the things kids say or do as much as their Mom and Dad. After the death of one parent, the other parent has to learn to enjoy her children alone, and it takes a lot of the fun out of it for a while. It also makes the problems we have with our children harder to handle when we are totally responsible for them. This is another area of adjustment—one that becomes easier to do the longer we do it.

Don't worry if you go through a period when you hate your kids. This too will pass. Many widows have known such a period. A widow told me in front of another friend that she hated her kids right after her husband died. Her other friend was horrified, but I wasn't. As reality set in for me, I found myself resenting my children. I told myself I didn't want their love—I wanted Bob's. I didn't want *anybody's* love but Bob's. This phase never lasts long. A much more serious problem exists when widowed parents let themselves become *too* involved with their children and do not have any social life away from them.

People will sometimes forget that your children do not have both parents and will make comments that hurt them, just as people hurt us when they talk about husbands. Teachers are especially careless in this regard, and will frequently make general statements about parents, such as: "Tell your mother and father to take you to the museum," or "Print 'I love you, Mommy and Daddy' on the valentine." One day, Jan came home simply crushed because the teacher had gone around the room asking each of the children to say what their Dads did for a living. (I thought the teacher's prying was unbelievably crude to begin with!) When she got to Jan, she still didn't remember that Jan didn't have a Daddy, so Jan had to stand up and tell the whole class that her Daddy was dead. Jan was actually sick over it when she got home, and it took all my willpower not to go break the teacher's neck. If one of your children's teachers is tactless in this regard, *tell her about it.* She probably has no idea she is hurting your child, and a word from you on the subject will help other single-parent children.

Naturally kids get jealous too. Even now, Jan will come home feeling blue occasionally because the kids talked about their Dads at school lunch. When she stays overnight with a friend and sees a "whole" family together, she is reminded of what she is missing, and she feels shortchanged. Tell your kids what you tell yourself about jealousy: it's normal, but it isn't any fun, so try not to be jealous.

Being around other children who have single parents will make your children feel better. When you find that friend who's been there, if she has children, do things that involve your children and hers. Even though they may not talk about their grief as a result, they will all feel less "different" and there will be an unspoken bond between them because of their understanding one another's situation.

It will help you *and* your kids if you do things together. It will make some happiness happen for them and you—so bike, hike, swim, fish, play cards; go on picnics, to movies, ballgames, church; travel, watch TV, bake cookies, work around the house or yard together, bowl, play games (from tiddlywinks to chess); go camping, skating, skiing, sledding, horseback riding. Togetherness pays off for everyone concerned.

It isn't easy bringing up children with *two* parents working at it, and the responsibility of doing it alone may cause you to panic. Children make life much less lonely for a widow, however, and give us a purpose for living during that period when we feel we have lost all other reason for doing so. Children give widows additional problems, however, and tie us down. It is almost impossible to leave the children to go on a vacation when they are small, and even harder to do so when they are teenagers. We get tired of being both a mother and a father; it is exhausting and demanding.

If possible, it is a good practice to get away from your kids for a few days occasionally. Even a few *hours* will help, if you can't get away for a longer time. It does wonders for you *and* for the kids! It puts your life into a better perspective. They will be glad to see you go, and will be even happier to see you come back—and vice versa. When you are away from them, you will renew your appreciation of how much you love them and how important they are to you—and again, vice versa.

Widows I've talked to whose "last" child was about to leave home were usually very apprehensive about being left alone. They felt fortunate to have had children at home when their husbands died, and dreaded having the children leave. But in each case, they found that they also felt relieved of responsibility after that last child left home; the sense of relief compensated for the added loneliness of living by themselves.

One woman who had had a large family said she loved the freedom of living alone after all her children had "left the nest." After waiting on her family for years, she enjoyed not having to prepare meals on time and not having to pick up after anyone but herself.

Men and women who will not consider marrying again while their children are still at home, often do so after their children are grown.

So children seem to be both an advantage and a disadvantage to the widowed.

I wish my children had not lost their father. It hurts me terribly to think of the love they have missed. It isn't fair; but life is not fair.

There is no doubt that grief has changed my children—just as it changes all of us—but I have no way of knowing whether it has helped or hurt their characters and personalities. They have certainly had to learn many hard lessons about life and people that others sometimes do not learn until they are middle-aged. It affected their happiness for a time, but now they seem to be as happy as any other children their age who have both parents.

We cannot change the situation for our children, but because "they are people too," we should let them grieve appropriately and help them adjust to life with one parent.

CHAPTER THIRTEEN

Money Is a Dirty Word

FOR MOST widows, *money* is a dirty word either because of their lack of it, or because of their getting it the hard way, in death benefits.

The majority of widows have big financial worries. Elderly widows are the poorest group of people in America—poorer than blacks and migrant workers. Too old to work or even to get employment if they are physically *able* to work, these older women have to struggle to survive from day to day. Up till a given age (which is subject to the decision of Congress), they are usually not entitled to Social Security benefits and are often forced to live an impoverished lifestyle compared to what they enjoyed before the death of their husbands.

On the other hand, some widows inherit comfortable to large incomes, insurance, and other death benefits from their husbands. Most widows must live on what they can earn. Since many widows have not been gainfully employed, or trained in well-paid fields, they often find it difficult to support themselves. Widows who have worked outside the home all their lives generally continue to work after the death of their husbands, and generally at well-paying jobs. Their income is seldom equal to that of their husband, however. Recent statistics show that the average male *high school drop-out* makes more money than a female *college graduate*.

Every widow, especially if she still has minor children living at home, should contact a local office of the Social Security Administration to find out what financial support she is entitled to.

Peggy and I were fortunate. We had both worked all our married lives and had fairly good jobs. We had also received some insurance money. She received Social Security benefits for her children, and I received an annuity from Bob's Civil Service Retirement for my children.

We both had a strange difficulty in coping with the insurance money. We had had to pinch pennies for a part of our married lives, and now the rainfall of insurance money, without our husbands there to share it with us, was galling. I think we thought of it as "blood money"—as though Fate had put money in the bank "in trade" for our husbands—and we thought it was a rotten deal. Money in the bank can be a cold pain in the pit of your stomach when there is no one with whom to do the things extra money makes possible. We had no one to go house-hunting with for a dream home. No one to go on trips with. No place to wear new clothes.

A *lack* of money is, of course, far worse. Many of the widows I've talked to have had a hard time making ends meet, and couldn't possibly have done so if they had not gone to work. Some had never before had to work outside the home.

Some widows managed, or helped manage, the family finances before their husbands died. Many more, however, had never done so before. My own mother was an example of the latter. She got headaches trying to balance her checking account after my father died. She was an intelligent woman, but my father had handled all the money matters, so she had never had any experience managing money until she was widowed at the age of seventy! She never developed confidence in making financial decisions without the help of her children, and to her dying day she viewed her checkbook as her mortal enemy and considered it a personal affront that it never balanced.

Many women who begin managing financial affairs for the first time when they are widowed take to it like ducks to water, though, and enjoy it. Most of us are apprehensive about making financial decisions on our own at first, but gradually we develop self-confidence about it, and we recognize that one of the advantages to being a widow is to be able to spend money without anyone else's approval.

Some widows whose income changed drastically after they were widowed became bitter and resentful that their husbands had not provided for them by taking out adequate insurance or investing wisely. They found it extremely difficult to go to work outside the home after not having been employed for years. But once they got jobs and were working for a while, they found their work challenging, as well as interesting and financially rewarding. Many widows who do not need the money to live on take a job in order to be with people and to give themselves a "purpose" in life.

Decisions about money or anything else are a major problem for the new widow at first because her grief confuses her and she is not used to making decisions alone.

Think a problem over carefully before you do anything. Ask advice of family and friends; *then do what you think is best.* Don't go back and rehash all the pros and cons *after you have made the decision.* If you find out later you made the wrong decision, have no regrets about it, because you did the best you could do at the time.

Important financial decisions should be thought out very carefully. Whenever possible, *avoid making an important decision in a hurry.* It isn't always possible to postpone a decision, however. I had to sell one of our cars right away. Peggy had to sell her husband's boat. A farmer's wife had to sell their farm equipment immediately after her husband died rather than let it depreciate through the winter months.

A good yardstick to go by is: Don't do anything for the first year—*unless you have to*. Buying or selling property definitely falls into that category. So does moving. You can't wait a year to fix a leaking roof, however, and you can't leave the insurance money in a sock for a year.

One of the safest places to get advice about your finances is at your bank. A trust officer at the bank will give you suggestions on how to handle your monies and investments, and even help you make your will with the aid of your lawyer. He will discuss various types of investments with you in plain language you can understand.

Some wealthy widows are so insecure about money that they are afraid to spend any, even though they have scads of it. A trust officer will explain how much money you can spend without jeopardizing your security.

A help in decision-making is to make a list of the pros and cons involved. Seeing them written down in black and white helps you identify and weigh the advantages and disadvantages, and you are more apt to make the "right" decision.

When I was thinking of moving from West Virginia to South Dakota, I made out the following list and came to the conclusion—on paper and in my mind—that it would be best for me to move:

Pros

1. Family there to take care of the kids if I get sick.
2. It's safe to live alone there. I'm afraid here.

3. It would be easier to get together with friends in a small town.

4. It's easier to meet new friends in a small town.

5. The kids could walk to school.

6. Remodeling that old house would give me something to think about.

7. The family would provide moral support for me and father-figures for the kids.

8. I can always move back if I don't like it there.

Cons

1. We'd miss Bob's mother and all our friends here.

2. We'd miss W. Va. We love it here. It's home.

3. I like my job and the people I work with.

4. South Dakota's climate can't compare to W. Va.'s.

5. Milbank is a strange town after all these years. I don't know anyone there except family.

6. I'll never find a job in Milbank that pays as well as the one I have.

7. You have no privacy in a small town.

8. The kids could go to college in Huntington.

9. There's more to do in a city.

That list of pros and cons helped me to decide that I would be happier if I moved. The same list might have helped someone else come to the decision that it would be foolish to move —depending on *her* priorities.

Going to work is a major decision for widows. Many of them have to go to work to support themselves, and do not know how to go about it. If you are thrown into job-seeking at age forty or older, particularly if you have never worked before, you will run into a number of problems. Go to your local state employment office for help. You may wish to obtain information about vocational education schools in your area. A directory of schools can be obtained without charge from NATTS, 2021 L Street N.W., Washington, D.C. 20036.

You have talents and abilities that qualify you for some type of employment, and you can be trained for other types. One woman I know took a secretarial course when she was fifty and went to work in an office. Another went to work in the kitchen of a hospital; another, as a cook for the school lunch program; another, as a waitress; another cleaned house for couples who worked; another babysat in her own home.

Some women got part-time jobs; others, full-time. Many with past experience obtained jobs with good salaries immediately in their field as office workers, nurses, teachers, and so on. Others started small businesses. It is interesting that *the majority of widows say they enjoy working.*

Bill Rafferty, a counselor with the Michigan Employment Office in Detroit, offers the following advice to the widowed or divorced woman over forty-five who has not previously been employed. First, take a realistic look at yourself and determine what you can and what you cannot do. *You can do something.* Second, other people can guide and advise you, but remember that *you are responsible for finding the right job for you.* Third, after you get advice and guidance, put it all together yourself, develop a plan, and then "damn the torpedoes, full speed ahead" with your plan!

Be responsible *yourself* for what happens. Use other people for ideas, but don't depend on them to find the right job for you. *Depend on yourself.*

Be patient about finding the right job that fits your realistic appraisal of your abilities. Do not expect to start at the top. There are no overnight miracles. Sometimes it is a good idea to get a menial job in a large organization and plan from there. For example: get a job as a cook in the kitchen of a hospital. Then look around at the other jobs in the hospital and see if there is one you would like. You might want to be a nurse's aide, a nurse, or an office worker. Go to school on your off-hours to qualify yourself for the job you want, so that when there is an opening you can be transferred to it.

Rafferty cautions women to "expect some hard knocks" but not get "discouraged or depressed along the way." Louis Pasteur vowed he would build his success on three words: *will, work, wait.* I have heard innumerable "success" stories about widows who started at the bottom and worked their way up to exciting, successful careers.

Whether you have to work for money in order to pay your bills or in order to be with people so as to overcome your loneliness, work is good therapy and can help you build a good self-image as an individual, which in turn produces strong feelings of satisfaction and contentment.

If you feel abused about having to work, or are bored with your job, read O. A. Battista's *How to Enjoy Work and Get More Fun Out of Life* (1962). We all go through periods of hating to go to work. Dr. Battista has some excellent ideas to keep you happy and relaxed on the job and to help get you promoted. He will make you enthusiastic about your job and show you how to handle pressures at home and on the job.

Financial pressure is painful, to put it mildly. Stretching your dollars can ease the pain, and you may find some of the following suggestions helpful if you aren't already using them—*and more!*

If at all possible, start a *savings plan*, no matter how small. Payroll savings plans are the easiest way to save money. There are always a dozen places in which you could spend your entire paycheck; but if you don't get all your pay in your grubby little fist, you probably will be able to make the amount you do "take home" stretch to fit your needs. Even $5.00 saved each week can add up to *something* in a sock for a rainy day, which is better than *nothing*. When you get a raise, try to increase the amount you put in savings each week. You will be surprised at how fast even a small weekly amount will grow into a sizable nest egg.

Bob and I bought used furniture and appliances when we were first married, and I still buy used items whenever possible. Check used items over carefully, of course, before buying them.

You can buy "like new" things for pennies at garage sales, things that would cost ten to fifty times as much if purchased new. Sometimes the items available at such sales have never been used.

Packing your lunch and eating in the lounge at work, instead of buying lunch at a cafeteria, will save you more than you will believe. Figure up what you would save in a week and see for yourself. Making your own lunch also will help you keep track of calories and lose pounds, if you are watching your weight. Take a thermos of coffee to work for your coffee breaks too, instead of paying (too much!) for it from the vending machine.

All work and no play, of course, will make you miserable fast. If you have children and can't afford a babysitter, "trade" sitting time with another mother, preferably one with the same number of children as you have and approximately the same ages. This arrangement works, and saves everybody money.

Entertainment (which I'll talk about in more detail in the next chapter) comes cheap or expensive. Anyone can afford an evening playing cards with friends and serving coffee and cookies or beer and popcorn. Picnics in the park, bike riding, and just plain hiking are all fun—and cheap.

Sewing can probably save you more than any other money-saving project, and can be an enjoyable pastime. The advice, "If you want a boyfriend, dress as if you already have one," can be followed even if you are pinching pennies and making your own clothes. Thanks to the easy sewing patterns these days, you don't have to be an expert to make attractive clothes for the whole family. Buy a used sewing machine if you can't afford a new one. Sewing machines seldom wear out, and you don't need *all* those fancy stitches available on the new machines. My machine is 30 years old and has had hard usage, but it runs like a top. If a machine sews backward and forward and makes buttonholes, you can make almost any garment on it.

Buy your material on sale, off-season, for the coming year. Trade patterns with friends. They're expensive, and no one minds lending them. Look in shop windows and combine patterns to create your own clothes, or copy an expensive creation you can't afford to buy.

Sewing classes are a good investment. If you become an expert, you may be wise to invest in a more versatile and expensive machine. One woman I know, with a large family, makes all the clothes for her family, including her daughers' bathing suits and her son's leisure suits.

A West Virginia widow made a bold decision that has saved her a great deal of money. She sold her car and now walks or takes a bus or taxi wherever she goes. She claims that walking keeps her trim; she has saved enough money in gas, car insurance, and repairs to allow her to go on terrific vacations every year, despite her slim budget.

The do-it-yourself game also can save you money and accomplish a multitude of goals at the same time. (1) You will enjoy it, if you go into it with the idea that you are going to enjoy it, rather than feel sorry for yourself because you can't afford to hire the work done. (2) You will improve your self-image by doing repairs and improvements yourself, and (3) you will appreciate the results.

Wallpaper and paint can transform your surroundings and make you happier with the world in general. The same is true of new curtains, bedspreads, and drapes you make yourself. Decorating will help you become completey tuned into the *now*—and you will be looking forward to the future when you get your next project under way.

There are books put out by the U.S. government to help people budget their money and decide whether to buy or rent a home—common problems of the widowed or divorced woman. Three of these books are: *A Guide to Budgeting for the Family* (30¢), *Rent or Buy* ($1.40), and a pamphlet called *Wise Home Buying* (free) for those who decide to buy. All are available through the U.S. Government Printing Office, Superintendent of Documents, Washington, D.C. 20402. They are easy to understand and can save you money, blood, sweat, and tears if you read them carefully and follow their advice.

Meager incomes can be stretched with ingenuity. An 84-year-old widow wrote a newspaper article in which she described her life as "very full and rich" in spite of living alone in a low-rent housing development on a very limited income. She sympathized with lonely people, but said she wanted to tell them, "It's your own fault, you know" for not learning some handcrafts or acquiring some hobbies to fill in empty hours; for not making new friends to replace those who had died or moved away; for not having people over for cards or games and just serving coffee or tea, as "we all eat too much sweet stuff anyway."

Some of her own solutions for happiness and economy were: making good use of the public library for books and magazines; going to church social functions; cooking with the cheapest of foods instead of the highest priced (she even makes her own bread); raising plants inside in the winter and planting flowers outside in the summer; watching a black-and-white TV; walking for exercise and stopping to talk to people she saw on the way; attending Bible Study classes; being secretary of a garden club and devotions chairman of her church group. She claimed that almost anyone could make "a rich and satisfying life from bits and pieces, life's broken bottles and driftwood—if they only worked at it a bit."

CHAPTER FOURTEEN

Try Almost Anything Twice

Y O U   D O not *have* to take any steps to make yourself happier, but the world will *not* come to you; so if you want to be happy, you are going to have to go out to meet the world.

In Chinese, the word for "crisis" means both a danger and an opportunity. Being widowed is a major crisis, one that endangers the rest of your life. It is also an opportunity and a challenge to make the most of a difficult situation. It is an opportunity to create a new life for yourself that *could* bring you joys you have never before experienced. To create a new life, however, you must be willing to try new things.

Unfortunately, we don't want to give anything a try when we are depressed. We do the same thing our kids do when they are bored; no matter what we suggest they do, *they have a reason for not doing it.* In *Games People Play,* Eric Berne calls this behavior the "Why don't you—Yes but" game. I played this game to the hilt, and I hear others play it constantly. Not only the widowed, but men, women, and children who complain of boredom but refuse to take the responsibility upon themselves for making something interesting happen.

I am sure you will recognize yourself in this typical example of how we play the game with a friend or relative who is trying to help us:

Friend: Let's go bowling.
You: I don't feel like it.
Friend: Why don't we get up a bridge foursome?
You: I'm a rotten bridge player.
Friend: The hospital auxiliary could use some more members. Why not join?
You: I hate hospitals. They depress me.
Friend: Why not take golf lessons and join a league?
You: The sun is bad for your skin.
Friend: How about going on a picnic Sunday?
You: I don't care much for picnics.
Friend: Let's go to ceramics class next Tuesday.
You: No thanks. There'd just be a lot of old women there.

This game often goes on like that for hours, with your friends and relatives trying to pry you out of your depression and push you back into the world of the living. If they do manage to blast you out of your lethargy, you will be sure, *before* you go, that you aren't going to like it! If you do go someplace and do something, however, you are bound to have more fun than if you had stayed at home. You are nevertheless apt to go back to manufacturing excuses for not making an effort to overcome your misery, and again refuse to budge from the house for any reason.

You are not "basking in your misery," as some people may think. This is typical behavior for a depressed person, particularly the bereaved. If you are depressed, try to talk yourself into doing something—*anything*—with others. Go to church, to a school play, or to the park; visit a friend. Get involved with people in groups or individually. It will bring you happiness. I promise.

Think of happiness as a measurable quantity, like a cube of sugar. Each cube is a unit of happiness. Having coffee with a friend could be anywhere from one cube of happiness to twenty cubes—depending on how you feel about the friend and how much you enjoy his or her company. Laughter adds lots of happiness units to a situation; on the other hand, a serious talk with someone on music, for instance, or even on the state of the nation could also produce innumerable units of happiness for you, without any laughter.

I don't think most people are aware of how much happiness comes their way in an average day of their lives—from a phone call, a TV show they enjoyed, a book or article they read, or a sunset or rainstorm. Happiness in one form or another comes to all of us every day, but many of us are not aware of it. The most important thing about happiness is to appreciate it when it comes your way!

We need other people, at least a part of the time, to help us to be happy. It's a two-way street called friendship, or mutual need. You need others to help *you* to be happy, and others need you to help *them* to be happy. If you have a group over for cards, your friends have a nice evening, and so do you.

It even works in business. A restaurant owner I know makes a practice of asking widows to work for him. He knows that it is good for them to get out with other people, and that they probably need the wages; and he can use good, reliable employees. Mutual need works beautifully for all concerned.

We need others, but we are often too lazy to push ourselves into doing things. We are inclined to wait for someone else to make the arrangements for a card game or a covered-dish dinner, and we are very hesitant to try anything new. James H. Jauncey, in *Above Ourselves*, writes: "Many wealthy people are desperately unhappy and many poor people are supremely content. Our main enemy is human inertia, or plain laziness. The possibility of recapturing zest in living is always there. Fear of failing and laziness are our enemies."

You are in charge of every minute of your life. You and no one else. It is up to you to decide how you want to spend each minute, *and whether or not you want to appreciate each as it comes.* Ralph Waldo Emerson wrote, "Each moment has its own beauty—a picture which was never seen before and which shall never be seen again." No matter what our circumstances, we can be aware of the beauty around us and appreciate the gift of life with its spectrum of joys and sorrows, friends and activities.

Getting involved with others is difficult for you to do on your own after having been married. There is also an element of risk involved, as we well know. In *I Heard the Owl Call My Name,* Margaret Cravens writes of the lonely school teacher: "In his tiny house the teacher heard the running footfalls on the path to the river bank, and he went quickly to the door but could not open it. To join the others was to care, and to care was to live and to suffer." We find fulfillment and happiness when we work through our grief and bitterness and are willing once again to risk involvement with others, with its consequences of love *and* pain.

Friends are all-important to happiness. Keep your old friends, but be constantly open to new friendships. Michel Quoist notes, in *The Meaning of Success,* that

today we are witnesses to an almost universal urge—both on the part of individuals and of nations—to establish contact with others. Some hold this to be an absolute necessity, others a duty. It is both. It is a necessity because no man is an island sufficient unto himself, it is a duty because man cannot attain self-fulfillment unless he becomes one with all men. If you really want to establish contact with another you have to be genuinely interested in his *(or her)* work, *his* family, *his* likes, *his* aspirations, *his* difficulties, *his* struggles. *You must sincerely desire to know him so that you can come to understand and to love him.*

To be a good friend, we must be interested in others. The happiest people I know are involved in numerous activities with various types of people. Many people become interested in a favorite charity or "cause" through a sense of duty or an urge for self-fulfillment. I have seen strange things happen to people who get involved in causes. They generally go into it with the idea of helping others, which they do, but in the process they derive great satisfaction and pleasure from working with others toward a common goal.

Jerry Lewis and Eunice Shriver are examples of this motivation in their work with the Muscular Dystrophy and Retarded Children organizations. They probably began their work through a sense of duty to humanity. It is obvious, however, that it is no longer a sense of duty that drives them to work tirelessly for these causes. It is an absorbing, exciting activity for them. Bob Hope and his compassionate Christmas trips to entertain servicemen all over the world is another example of the obvious personal pleasure a cause brings to an individual, along with its heavy demands physically and emotionally. One friend can be an exciting experience. Lewis, Shriver, and Hope have made thousands of wonderful friendships as a result of what probably started out as a sense of duty.

Hunt around. Find something you are interested in—whether it is promoting a plant-a-tree program or a duplicate bridge club—and get involved. Two years ago, I volunteered to be treasurer of a church group because no one else would do it, and I got interested in spite of myself. I got so involved that I met myself going and coming to meetings; I also met terrific young, old, and middle-aged people I would never have gotten to know otherwise.

Going to work is another good way to get yourself involved with others. It puts money in your pocket, and it gives you a regular routine, a reason for getting up in the morning, and a sense of accomplishment. Many widows told me they would have "gone nuts" if they hadn't gone to work. They felt their jobs had literally been lifesavers for them. Working improves your self-image; you will get to know your co-workers well; you will have things in common to talk about (including griping about the boss!); and you will find yourself sharing confidences, as well as laughs, with others. Many of my closest friends all my life have been people I have met at work.

People ask what groups to join and what to do. The list is endless, of course, and your own interests will determine what possibilities you should investigate. There are all the health associations to promote research and aid people with heart disease, cancer, muscular dystrophy, multiple sclerosis, crippled children, the retarded, and the mentally ill. Go through your local phone book and pick one you are interested in. Go to a few meetings to see if you like the people and the organization. If you don't enjoy yourself after a few meetings, *quit*, and try another.

Your church *always* needs willing workers. Join a hiking, birdwatchers', or duplicate bridge club. Join a bowling or golf league, ceramics class, or gardening club.

There are all sorts of learning situations you may want to get into, where you will meet others who are interested in the same thing you are. Beginner's bridge lessons, for example, or classes in golf, skiing, sewing, upholstering, flower arranging, carpentry, or car repair, to name a few.

If you live in a college town, courses are available day and night on anything and everything imaginable. The same is true of most high schools and trade schools. Check into the many educational opportunities in your area and see what they have to offer you. You'll meet interesting people, as well as add to your knowledge and skills.

Some activities can be pursued that will enrich the time you spend alone. Music is a fascinating area to explore. Few of us have more than skimmed the surface in developing an ability to appreciate different types of music. Borrow recordings from the public library and trade your own recordings with friends.

Reading can be, and is, a full-time hobby for many people, young and old. I reread *Huckleberry Finn* recently and discovered that Mark Twain's humor had been wasted on me as a child. Librarians are willing and anxious to help you select books of the type you prefer; friends will exchange books with you and share their recommendations.

Music and literature do not exhaust the list of things you can do alone. If you can't find someone to go with you, or want to go on the spur of the moment, hike, bike, swim, or cross-country ski alone. Many people have bird feeders in their yards and birdwatch the year around from their living rooms. Young and old people are raising plants these days—a hobby that you can enjoy alone and also discuss at length with other plant growers. Watch TV. The educational channels offer marvelous dramatizations of the classics in serial form. Make candles. Work jigsaw or crossword puzzles. Grow herbs and give them to your friends for Christmas; they'll love you for it.

You can work hard at accumulating cubes of happiness, or you can come by them easily while reading the morning paper, sitting on your front porch with a cup of coffee at your elbow. One of my co-workers got up two hours early every morning so she could read her paper and drink coffee while soaking in the tub! She said it was the happiest part of her day and that she couldn't have faced a day at work without first having that period of relaxation.

Choose activities that fit into your schedule. If you are afraid to go out alone at night, join groups that meet in the daytime. If you are working, look into weekend or evening activities. Our local Mental Health Association has noon luncheon meetings so that business people can come. Their schedule fits mine perfectly because Jan and Leigh Ann have lunch at school.

The larger the town you live in, the larger selection you will have of organizations from which to choose. There are singles groups in most large cities and in many small towns. I belonged to a singles club for a year or so and enjoyed it very much. My membership was during that period when I felt more comfortable with single people because seeing married couples together made me more lonesome for Bob and more conscious of being alone. I had to force myself to go at first, but convinced myself it was better to go than to sit home alone—and it was. Later I gradually became active in groups with married and single people in them. I now belong to a widowed-and-divorced support group and think it is terrific. The sharing of ideas within the group makes it more interesting and helpful, in my estimation, than the singles groups, which exist primarily or solely for entertainment purposes.

From a widow's point of view, the main drawback to singles groups is that the women members far outnumber the men; this imbalance makes for an uncomfortable situation if you do not have a good self-image, and it may accentuate your feelings of loneliness. Our support-group members enjoy discussing *women's* problems in the widowed and divorced situation so much that some of the women wanted to tell the men to start their own group; but that proposal was outvoted. I saw a notice in a Minneapolis paper recently for a workshop for single people called "Creative Contacts for Singles," and attendance was limited to the first 100 men *and* 100 women who made reservations. Some singles cruises are handled this way also, I understand.

More and more churches are sponsoring activities for single, widowed, and divorced people; these activities, I've found, are especially comfortable because of the setting.

For heaven's sake, don't avoid singles groups because you are ashamed of being "one of them," or because you feel "better" than they are. That attitude about ourselves is what makes being single painful. When we singles accept ourselves, singles will have it made!

I see a healthy attitude developing among widowed and divorced people in support groups. *We are proud of ourselves*. We get together and appreciate and help one another. We all belong to other groups also that we enjoy, but a support group gives us something other groups do not, and we look forward to our meetings. Here again, of course, if you go to the meetings of such a group a few times and don't enjoy them, *quit*.

Everyone needs human companionship, but it takes effort on our part to be with others when we are single. A therapist counseled her patients to practice meeting ten people in order to acquire experience at it. It is especially hard for many women to meet people, because they have been taught that they should not be "aggressive." She advised people to be frank and sincere in talking to others, to ask questions about the other person; and then, too, after someone has told you about himself or herself, tell the person about yourself. She also advised single people *to go out alone occasionally, rather than always going out with a friend*, because it is easier to meet new friends that way.

Places and activities she suggested as likely ways of meeting people were: the bird sanctuary at the zoo, a park, a laundromat, hiking, bus stop, tennis club, political campaign, square dancing, American Legion convention, night classes at the college or university, club meetings, church meetings, art shows, dog shows, poetry readings, and lectures. Meeting people is not difficult at all, once you practice a bit.

If there is not a club in your town offering exactly what you are interested in, *start one!* People will thank you for it. Start a hiking club, for instance, or a biking, birdwatcher, yoga, finger-painting, gourmet cooking, think-thin cooking, or gardening club. If you have money to invest, start an investment club. Organize a group to protest bad television shows and applaud good ones. Start a rose or dandelion club. Don't sit back and wait for someone else to make things happen. Make them happen yourself.

A friend of mine, in her seventies, finds it very difficult to get out in the wintertime because of the snow and ice; but she loves and needs people, so she invites her friends over for coffee parties almost every day. If her friends have a house guest, she'll invite the house guest too. She is a vivacious, charming, brilliant woman, and her friends enjoy being invited and being with her. She's made it a practice all her life to make her own happiness happen.

Some apartment houses have recreation centers, which are a great help to getting acquainted with people. In looking for friends to do things with, don't forget the women whose husbands travel or work on irregular shifts. These women are glad to have a way to fill in *their* empty hours and will be delighted to be asked to go places with you. Most people will be overjoyed that you have gone to the trouble of making the necessary plans, because we all have that "inertia problem."

The diet clubs have always seemed to me to be enjoyable, so much so that I am almost tempted to gain weight so I can join one. Health-food clubs are also a great opportunity to meet people who are enthusiastic about a common interest.

Happiness often depends on how enthusiastic we are about things and people around us. When you become enthusiastic about *anything*, from antiques to stamp collecting, you will find yourself too busy enjoying life to bother to compare your life with that of others who may be more fortunate than you are. Enthusiasm is contagious—just as contagious as depression, but much more fun!

Try to make every day of your life happy. Even the bad days should have *some* happy minutes in them if you are making an honest effort to try to be happy. Lining your cupboard shelves with bright paper can be a happy task; so can filling out a new address book, or buying a new towel rack and putting it up yourself. Your efforts don't have to be grand and glorious to reap satisfaction and enjoyment for yourself.

Some Michigan widows formed a club to *force* one another to go out. They make plans to go places and do interesting things together; and they won't take "no" for an answer from any member, because they all know how easy it is to back out at the last minute and stay home alone and blue.

If you do not make an effort to reach out for new friends and interests, *your life will remain dull and uninteresting*. This rule holds true all our lives, but far more so when we are single. So give a party, take up growing your own bean sprouts, go to a concert in the park. . . . Any plus is better than a minus.

When you are depressed, you do not want to accept the responsibility for making a rich, full, happy life for yourself. To do so takes a great deal of effort. The choice, of course, is yours.

CHAPTER FIFTEEN

Anybody Seen
a Guy on a White Charger?

ONE NIGHT as we were assessing our suddenly unmarried situation, Peggy said, "Well, there's no point in dreaming about a knight on a white charger coming along to save us at our age." Knights on white chargers are hard to find at any age, and become scarcer the older a woman gets. The fact that there are far more single women in the world than single men is probably the widow's most frustrating problem, since neither man *nor woman* was meant to live alone.

Once a widower or divorced man is over the raw hurt of losing his wife, if he is willing to make the effort to look for one, he can find himself another wife because there are so many single women "available." Men often find it difficult to get into the dating game after being away from it for years; but the intensity of their loneliness usually is strong, and most soon marry again.

One man described the usual situation when he said that after his mother died, his father "grieved, of course, but later he had a great time dating lots of women; was wined and dined by them for a couple of years before he married one of the women, and seems to be quite happy now."

Counselors advise widowers to date several women before they pick a second wife. I wish I could similarly advise widows to date several men before they choose a second husband. But the truth is that many widows don't ever get the chance to date at all. After we get over our sorrow, many or most of us must continue to live alone; that is an abnormal life for us and one that most of us would not choose, if we had a choice. The continual adjustment to living alone actually requires greater effort from us than overcoming our sorrow does.

No matter what your age might be, if you prefer being married to being single, keep on looking for Mr. Right Guy to come along, just as you did before you were married the first time. The odds aren't *very* favorable that he will, but it happens all the time, in spite of the odds, and it could happen to you.

Don't let other people, most of whom are married themselves, make you feel you are peculiar if you are interested in meeting eligible men in the hope that you will fall in love and marry again. It would be *more* peculiar if you were *not* interested in the opposite sex.

Join organizations and church groups whose

membership includes men. Take adult-education classes. Go to work in a motel, or in a factory that employs a great many men, or as a waitress in a restaurant. Get involved in local politics and community affairs. *Go where the men are.*

I wish all of us widows had the opportunity to date, because it builds up a self-image faster than anything else does. A large part of our self-image problem is the fact that society encourages men and women to "pair off" as couples, so that not having a spouse or a "boyfriend" cuts down our self-image, and makes us feel inferior.

It is totally illogical to think that dating or not dating—or, for that matter, being married or unmarried—makes a person either superior or inferior. After dating a few times, widows generally get over the feeling that it is important to their self-image to be seen with a man and are only interested in dating from a normal attraction to the opposite sex, and a desire to socialize in mixed groups.

If you get the chance to date, ignore the noble souls who suggest or imply that you should show your "devotion" to your deceased spouse for a "decent length of time." This is a ridiculous attitude. They haven't been down your lonely road themselves, and don't know what it's like, so turn a deaf ear to them and date if the opportunity presents itself and you yourself would like to. Dating certainly can make life more interesting for you—and that's a plus.

Some widows are so lonely they will go out

with any man they meet. Others are so choosey they would rather stay home than go out with a man who is not their "type." Most widowed and divorced men and women dislike living alone, and would like to meet a compatible person and remarry. One old man I knew was still terribly bitter years after his wife died. When I made my usual comment, "Widowed is lonely, isn't it?" he snatched a Bible from a table and threw it back down again, shouting as he did so, "Man was not meant to be alone! That G-- d--- book *says so!*" Yet at my suggestion that he join the senior citizen group in town to meet some nice women, he said he had tried it and all they did was play cards. He made it plain that he was looking for another wife, and was very lonely; but the last I heard of him, he was still single—and probably still cussing the Lord about it.

One woman I met had no difficulty finding men to marry. Her first husband was a big, good-looking executive. Within a year after he died, she married a janitor, a plain man about half her size. He died ten years later, and again she wasted no time. Within six months she married a truck driver. She doesn't go around crying about yesterday. She's too busy living today.

If you go to some effort to go places and do things where the men are, in all likelihood you will find someone to date. And dating will put you back into a normal, affectionate man-woman relationship. A few months after Bob died, one of my brothers came to visit me. He kissed me and hugged me close, saying without words how much it hurt him to see me hurt, and how much he loved me. It felt wonderful to be held in a man's loving embrace again. The strength of his arms and the security of his love gave me more support than a million words could have done. We all need affection, and dating is one way of getting it.

Adjusting to a celibate life after being married is one of the difficult areas of adjustment forced upon the widowed; an area often cruelly misconstrued by others. Many widows complain of men making sexual advances when they began dating, and many widowers complain of sexually aggressive women!

Those of us who believe that sexual intercourse outside of marriage is wrong will probably run into some pressure to "join the crowd." What puzzles me is that "modern thinkers" talk so much about our "right" to have sex outside of marriage that I get the impression that they don't think we have the "right" *not* to indulge in it if we feel it is wrong! Don't let anyone talk you into it because "everybody is doing it these days." Everybody isn't. Most men will admire you if you stick to your principles, but more important than their admiration is the fact that you will be happy with yourself. I found out as a kid in grade school, when "everybody" was smoking cigarettes out behind the garage, that guilt is harder to live with than frustration is. As an adult, I've learned that compromising on a matter of principle never makes you feel good about yourself.

If you had a normal sexual relationship with your husband, you will feel "frustrated" at home as well as on dates at times. The best advice I was given for coping with sexual energy was to do something strenuous immediately, no matter what time of the day or night. Go hiking or biking, scrub walls, wash windows, clean the refrigerator, mow the law, pull weeds, wash the car. Physical exertion will make you feel better *fast*. Rechanneled sexual energy can accomplish marvels!

We want to date because of our normal, healthy desire for love and human companionship. Meeting people to date is a problem for singles of all ages after they finish school. Singles groups often fall apart after the leaders get married, and have other disadvantages, as I mentioned earlier. The most effective group setting where older widows can meet eligible men seems to be Senior Citizens, where both married and single people are included and accepted. If all of society showed the same attitude of acceptance, much of the pain would vanish from being single.

Women in our culture have three big disadvantages in the dating game. (1) They outnumber men, especially as age-level rises. (2) It is not universally acceptable for them to go to some public places alone. (3) It is not universally acceptable for them to ask a man for a date.

The more I think about dating "rules," the more ridiculous they seem to be. Many young women have changed the rules, but many more young, and most older, women do not feel comfortable about altering them. It *should* be acceptable for a man or woman to go into public places and "talk to strangers." The trouble is that we women will first have to change our own attitude about it, then the attitude of the men we would meet there, and then the attitude of the "others" who would see us there.

For example, why can't a woman go to a cocktail lounge or nightclub for companionship or in the hope of meeting someone she would like to date? I know some women of all ages *and* with very high moral standards who already are doing so; and more "nice" women are doing it all the time. One woman I know, who has met some nice men this way, doesn't even drink alcoholic beverages.

You can get into couple-situations in a more socially acceptable way, however, if you are willing to change your attitudes and behavior. If you know a man whose company you would enjoy, call him and suggest you go out together. Maybe he is afraid to call you. Most (not *all*) men at all ages are flattered when women call them, as even self-confident men often find it difficult to ask a woman for a date, particularly for the first time.

The "platonic" (no-touch) friendship between men and women could be the cure for the "social frustation" that singles have in our couple-oriented society. Many young people are already having success with it these days. I think that friends of the opposite sex *should* feel free to call one another and make arrangements to go out for dinner or a show, for dancing or a company party for employees—*with each one paying his or her own way,* just as friends of the same sex do. They could even help each other meet other men and women to date, *since they would not be "dating" each other!* They would merely be socializing with a friend who happens to be of the opposite sex.

I tried out that kind of relationship not long ago, and it worked so well I intend to try it again. I was going to a benefit dinner with my relatives and commented to a single man-friend that I would see him there. He said he wasn't going because he didn't have anyone to go with and didn't want to go alone. I suggested that he meet me there and that we could sit together and each of us pay for our own meal and drinks. We had a great time and laughed ourselves sick discussing the "single scene" in Milbank.

While platonic friendships would be a boon for single men and women and are an excellent idea in theory, they are difficult to put into practice because of the hesitation both men and women have about getting involved in relationships from which it might be difficult to extricate themselves later if they wanted to do so. Men are particularly leery of the "designing" female and are apt to suspect that you do not honestly want "just a friend" instead of a sweetheart; and if you are *not* honest about it, a platonic friendship *will not work.* Even if you go into it honestly, there is also the danger that one or the other of you might become interested in being more than a platonic friend later. One of you is sure to get hurt if the change in the relationship is not mutual. But there is always emotional "risk" involved in friendships.

There is also the fact that your being seen with a man *friend* might lessen your chances of having another man, in whom you are interested romantically, call to ask you out. Basically, however, the platonic friendship has marvelous possibilities for single men and women because they can go places and do things together along with married and single couples without an obligation to each other besides forming a "couple" themselves—which is so "important" in our society. Try it. It may work very well for you too.

It's unfortunate that married couples so seldom invite single friends to their homes for social affairs. If a married couple does invite you to a party or a dinner, don't get upset if they "pair you off" with a jerk. You don't have to marry the guy; you have merely been invited over for the evening. I wonder if we singles are to blame for not being invited out more often because of our objecting to being paired with people who are not our "type."

Pairing off seems to be so important in our society that everybody, including the single person, seems to feel uncomfortable if we are invited someplace and do not have a "partner." A single man is invited out alone socially far more readily than a single woman. But men too are sometimes left out of mixed social affairs, even by their "best friends." I have never been able to understand the reason, particularly in the case of cocktail parties or open houses, where it would seem that singles could be included without discomfort on anyone's part; and the occasion could actually be more fun as a result, as people are people.

If we singles are really motivated to change this situation, we will include married and single people when we entertain—*exactly as we would want others to entertain and include us.* We could include any singles of the opposite sex we might be interested in dating or seeing as a friend, as well as single friends of the same sex and our married friends. We can't very well complain about the situation if we ourselves are not doing anything to try to improve it. Establish a precedent for others to follow.

Many singles do somehow meet one another and date. Some singles are anxious to marry again rather than live alone, and date with that goal in mind.

More and more single, widowed, and divorced people are entering into agreements to "go steady" or live together for years—one or both of them not caring enough about the other to accept the commitments and responsibilities of marriage, and preferring to be free to go their separate ways anytime they wish.

Many widows hesitate to marry again because they feel men are often merely looking for a housekeeper or mother for their children, rather than a woman to love and to cherish. Not many men like to cook or clean, and most find it extremely inconvenient not to have a woman around the house to do it for them. It seems that older men in particular are not as interested in love and companionship as they are in having a wife who could make them comfortable.

Men or women who date for any appreciable length of time usually decide to get married unless there is a good reason, such as poor health, for not doing so. As in a first marriage, you need to be realistic and honest about what you expect from a second marriage. The following examples illustrate that point.

One woman told me she had been widowed five years when she went on a blind date, and knew the man was the "right one" for her when she saw him walking up to the door. She said she hadn't had any hope of ever meeting anyone she could love again, "but you never know what life has in store for you right around the corner." She had been married three years when I talked to her, and she said she was far happier than she had been "the first time."

A woman in her forties told me she "had" to marry again after her husband died because of her strong sex drive. She met and married a man shortly afterward but divorced him within two years "because he was always demanding what he was paying for." Sex apparently was not as necessary to her as she had originally thought it was. A perfect example of jumping from the frying pan into the fire!

Another woman told me she married an older

man a few years after her first husband died but that it wasn't "at all like the first time, of course," apparently meaning she was not as happy as she had been the first time.

One couple in their sixties, a woman widowed for five yers and a man widowed for three years, had not dated anyone after their spouses died; and their children were worried about their obvious loneliness and depression. The man and woman lived hundreds of miles apart, but a mutual friend suggested they write to one another; as a result, they met and married within a year. After four years of mariage, they are reportedly "as happy as larks."

Many widows do not date at all, or go for long periods of time between occasional dates. I devised a technique for feeling better about it when I haven't had a date in ages. You may want to try it.

When you are out in public with women friends, look around at the couples there and ask yourself how many of those people look as if they are having as good a time together as you and your friends are having, or if you think they are any happier than you are, even though they may have more "reason" to be. This technique works so well that you may end up feeling sorry for them. I often do. So many couples look so *bored*. A friend of mine once sat in the booth next to one occupied by a married couple at a restaurant; the couple never exchanged one word all through lunch.

I am convinced that if we were single by choice, it would change our whole perspective. You may someday decide you prefer being single. Women have told me they had no desire to marry again; but most of us prefer being married. And to judge from the high percentage of people who are married, marriage is obviously the preferred lifestyle, particularly for people who have been married. So it wouldn't surprise me at all if you are now feeling as resentful about your "single" status as that old man who shouted at me that neither man (nor woman) was meant to be alone.

I wish those of us who prefer being married to being single could all find a nice guy, fall in love, and marry again. Statistics say that we won't *all* be that lucky, but who knows who might be around the corner waiting for us?

I, for one, however, am not sitting around waiting for him to come along, to enjoy my life. I agree with the attitude expressed in one of Neil Diamond's songs: "We'er *alive*, we might as well be glad" . . . whether we're married or single!

CHAPTER SIXTEEN

Happiness Is . . .

HAPPINESS is *a state of mind,* not a set of circumstances. And each of us must work our way to a happiness of our own making, based on our own interests, attitudes, and priorities.

Happiness for *me* is banging on my typewriter, watching the newscast and "Mork and Mindy" on TV, papering the inside of my cupboards, or driving down a lake road that reminds me of West Virginia. It's reading Erma Bombeck, *Winds of War,* and the Bible, and looking forward to reading all the other books on my reading list. It's having a long agenda of things I want to get done today—and then not doing any of them because something else came up, or because I decided to have a lazy day. It's talking about wheel alignment with Leigh Ann, writing letters to distant friends, painting the garage, or baking a cake. It's listening to Jan play the piano, going hiking alone, discussing antiques with Vera, going to an auction with Nellie, playing Spite and Malice with Sandy, going cross-country skiing with Evelyn, or working on a funeral dinner with the women in the parish. It's comparing kid problems with Joan by long-distance phone, playing bridge with June and Emma and Mary, going to lunch with Verna, listening to recorded music while I sew, or having coffee "at home" and "away" with anybody and everybody.

In other words, happiness for me is *living*. When I was in the depths of depression, I asked myself, "Is this all there is left in life for me?" Now I can't explain on paper my feeling of well-being and contentment—or my own astonishment at arriving at such a high level of happiness. I have some blue days—everybody does—but now when I have them, I know that "this too shall pass" and that I'll be happier than ever the next day for having had a blue day to compare it with.

My memories don't hurt anymore. I'm glad I have them. Dante moaned after Beatrice died, "There is no misery like the remembrance of having once been happy," but I prefer to think as Frankl does: "What you have experienced, no power on earth can take from you." We will always have our memories, both good and bad.

Life has consisted of a mixture of highs and lows in every stage of my life, just as it does for all of us. There were the joys and sorrows of the years of my childhood as part of a large family in a small, friendly community—traumatic *and* happy teenage years in a strange big city with a family reduced to a small number—twenty-four years of a far-from-perfect but beautiful marriage—years of wonderful, and sometimes trying, friendships and of experiences at work—years of fun and frustration as a parent.

What I have experienced, *both good and bad*, no power on earth can take from me, and I live in anticipation of what lies in store for me in the future. Pain and sorrow are inevitable, *but laughter and joy are also inevitable*—and much more apt to fill my life now that I know where to look for them, and how to help them happen.

Now instead of fighting the memories of having once been happy with Bob, I appreciate their importance. I see them in a light that shows me their true value. I am aware that my memories not only made that period of my life both happy and sad, but are the foundation for continuing a life built upon them. Those memories will always be a part of me and my children. They will always affect our way of life, our capacity to give love to and receive love from others. Bob helped us to become the people we are, so that in a way he is still living in us, and will live in our grandchildren someday. His attitudes, his interest in and love of people and music, fun and life, have become a part of the three of us and will continue to affect the people whose lives we touch.

Happiness or unhappiness frequently depends on how we react to changes in our lives. I constantly hear of married and single parents whose grown children leave home. Some of these parents *never* adjust, never make a new life for themselves. Others accept the change and their new way of life, developing new friends and interests to fill the void left by their children. I especially admire the single parent who is totally alone after "the children" leave home, yet who often "adjusts" better than married couples who still have each other.

Early in the game of observing others coping with grief, I decided I'd rather be a winner than a loser, because I saw that *the winners liked themselves.* I am convinced that my improved self-image is the primary reason for my feeling happy most of the time. My family tells me that I am a different person, more self-confident than I have ever been.

For years I was ashamed of being a widow. Now I am proud of being one of the widowed (and divorced) women who cope with life "alone"—and who enjoy life in spite of the disadvantages single women face in our society.

It isn't easy to develop a positive self-image as a single woman in our society. The stereotyped "ideal" woman is a wife and mother with a husband who supports her financially, makes decisions for her, and is supposed to be depended upon to make her life happy. Then she is suddenly alone, with no man to support her financially and emotionally. What happens? Her self-image collapses or evaporates into thin air! How can a woman feel worthwhile without a man if she's been taught since childhood that success and happiness for a woman require that she have a husband? Under these circumstances, it automatically follows that "no husband" equals "no self-image."

I can't *believe* that I once accepted that definition by which a woman's success and happiness depend upon her having a husband, but I did; and so do most women, until they wake up and see how illogical it is. Marriage is a great institution—I'm all for it—but marriage does not guarantee success or happiness, and s-i-n-g-l-e does not spell unhappiness, either. You can be happy or unhappy, whether you are married or single. And your marital status should have nothing whatever to do with your sense of self-worth!

You will eventually see—if you don't already—that you are the same person you always were, except that you are becoming more competent and self-sufficient. This fact *should* improve your self-image. But most of us have also been brainwashed into thinking that dependency upon a man is feminine: so that being independent—as a single woman is *forced* to be—is threatening to our self-image. (Some men, in the same way, *do* feel threatened by "independent" women, because men also have been trained to see their "role" in a stereotyped way that such women naturally challenge.)

We adjust and become happy again *when we feel good about ourselves as single, independent, competent women.* Forget all that nonsense you have been taught about a "helpless" woman being "feminine." A helpless woman is just incompetent! I know a 58-year-old married woman who has never written a check. Some wives have never traveled alone and are "lost" when their husbands play golf or watch football Sunday afternoons. That's "feminine"? The heck it is! These women live in a narrow world and have never tried thinking and making decisions for themselves.

Depression is more common among women than among men because women tend to take on a "dependent role" in marriage. Two primary causes of depression are (1) not being in control of one's life, and (2) not getting satisfaction or recognition for what one does. After being widowed or divorced, many or most women are sadly lacking in both of these critical areas. A wife is not in control of her life if her husband has always controlled it; and she therefore can feel recognition *only as a wife.*

As a widow works through her grief, the situation reverses itself as she gradually becomes in control of her life (often for the first time), and is recognized *on her own merits.* I have seen widows grieve painfully, but then emerge into more complete people than they have ever been before when they get in control of their lives.

You probably know other women forced into the labor market for the first time in their lives after being widowed or divorced, who have reared large families on a shoestring; women who went into businesses of their own; women who farmed alone, or took over their husbands' businesses, or went back to college to be trained for the better-paying jobs so they could support themselves and their families. The most "successful" part of these women's stories, I think, is that such women learn to enjoy life "alone" in spite of the disadvantages and frustration of being a single woman. These women are not merely tolerating their situation. They are enthusiastically leading vibrant, full, satisfying, *happy* lives. For example:

"Mary" works in an office and collects antiques for a shop of her own someday. Not long ago, her daughter complained that she never sees anything of her mother—because Mary keeps on the go and has friends galore who will drive a couple of hundred miles to go out for dinner or to an auction or antique show.

"Harriet" retired a year ago but hasn't had time to go on any trips yet because she's "firming things up at home first" and is busy taking bridge and swimming lessons, redecorating her home, and joining organizations.

"Sue" is working, attending college part-time, and putting her four children through college. Divorced twice, she is hesitant to marry again because "men become possessive and bossy and don't want to go out and have a good time with friends."

"Dorothy" took over the family business in Minneapolis when her husband died in 1955 and converted it from a company with severe financial problems into a very successful business, with annual sales exceeding $70 million! At age 70, she enjoys working so much that she has no plans to retire.

"Mildred," who considered marrying an old friend after her husband died, changed her mind when her friend insisted she "clean up" her colorful, earthy vocabulary. She decided to stay single and enjoy life. At age 68, she is taking art classes, has already had her own show, is also taking literature and calligraphy courses "for the fun of it"—in between hostessing regular neighborhood parties.

"Betty" retired two years ago and moved to a big city, where there is more to see and do. She has had opportunities to date but has passed them up because she says she is "getting selfish" and doesn't want to trade "occasional loneliness" for a man again.

"Lorraine" is 56, well-to-do, and has no children. She dates two or three different men, gives frequent large dinner parties, and travels often.

"Sallie" was widowed at 40. She clerked in a large department store and had many opportunities to date but did not until her children were grown, when she married a man from her church.

"Carrie" has several children and was miserable until she took control of her life, separated from her alcoholic husband, and got a job. She has worked hard to support her family in a happy, financially-secure environment ever since. It is obvious *who* did it all, and she receives the "recognition" we all need for a good self-image and self-satisfaction. She had such a loser for a husband that she has lost all interest in men and refuses dates.

"Vivian," in her eighties, has a marvelous sense of humor and is active in Senior Citizens and in her church. An avid reader, she belongs to two study clubs. She lives alone in a modest home but says she has everything she needs, including a man who calls on her regularly but whom she refuses to marry. She says, "It's different, of course, for you younger women." She loves people and sees many of them regularly; she claims she has never been happier in her life.

"JoAnn" and "Carol" each owns her own business, are best friends, and never miss anything going on in town, in between their trips in and out of the country. They're smart business women and can tell you where to invest—and when.

The list is endless of stories about women who are in control of their lives and responsible for their own good time; who enjoy life and people, and feel good about themselves.

Many of us would prefer being married again if we found a nice guy willing to marry us. But who knows if we would then be as happy? A woman I worked with years ago got married when she was forty and got divorced within a year. She had entertained and traveled a great deal as a "single" executive, and marriage clipped her wings and "smothered" her. I can understand that now, but I didn't understand it at the time; because back then I was sure that no woman could be happy unless she was married.

Actress Joan Fontaine chose to remain single after a life with three husbands and two children. She told a reporter, "I'm doing exactly what I want to do with no one to be responsible to. The best part of my life alone is that I no longer need to feel guilty. At last I have time to live for myself. Each day I can do what I want to do, and not have to please someone else. I tell women facing life alone that those years should be cherished. [They should] keep their opportunities alive and maintain an intellectual stimulus that will make their lives interesting."

Being single isn't all bad. It allows you to make decisions for yourself; to fix meals when you want to; to go out to eat when you want to; to go on a trip where *you* want to go, without consulting someone else; to wake up and go to bed when you want to; to stay out as late as you like; to watch what you want to watch on television; to buy what you want *when you want it* (if you have the money). If you cannot change your way of life, at least appreciate the advantages your way of life gives you.

It took me a long time to get over feeling alone and unwanted by society; but now I feel good about myself and am my own best friend! I have a feeling of belonging, as a person and as a widow, in the universe—of fitting into the community, my church, my family, and organizations. I have come to a new, entirely different concept and appreciation of life and interpersonal relationships from what I used to have. I have come to believe that our "purpose" in life is to try to make life a little happier *for ourselves and everyone around us,* not just for our own family and friends. This purpose can be achieved in many small ways: by a greeting to others in passing, a flower in a window box for others to enjoy, or a few dollars given to a worthy cause. But somehow, in some way, we are all responsible for building a better world for ourselves and others.

Peggy was rescued by a knight on a white charger. She and I both thought at first that that was the only way to go. Yet I was rescued by hundreds of people, and I wonder who is honestly the happier? I am not happy in the same way she is—as a wife again—but I am most certainly happy because of new friends, new interests, and new strengths I didn't ask for and didn't want, but that are exciting and challenging anyway now that I have them.

There's a song that goes, "Only love can break a heart and only love can mend it." That's true. Love between me and God and between me and other people has mended my broken heart and made life beautiful for me, as it will for you once you are willing to reach out to them.

I am deeply grateful for *all* my friends. Many couples I know never go places or do things with anyone except one another. Some of us did the same thing when we were married. But I cringe now when I see people living in that way. William

E. Hulme, in *Creative Loneliness*, warns, "If you put all your intimacy eggs into one basket, dependency develops. The other person, whether friend or mate, exerts too much control over your life. By establishing other friendships, you gain other channels for your intimacy needs, in case any one relationship becomes temporarily troubled or its channel blocked." We widows know that an all-absorbing relationship can be permanently blocked by death.

I still miss Bob. I'll always miss my loved ones who have died. I miss also my father's sage advice and dry sense of humor, and my mother's happy disposition and interest in everything I ever did. I especially miss Bob's constant companionship and affection. Life will never be the same for me without those people I have loved so dearly; but that doesn't mean that life is not good for me. Life is not the *same*, but it's terrific anyway!

No one will ever take the place of Bob or my parents in my life, nor of the other dear ones I have loved and lost; because *no one person can ever take the special place of another in our hearts*. Life, however, need not be empty without those loved ones. It is inconvenient having to reach outside our homes for the companionship and love we all need to survive, but I discovered, as you will, that happiness is "out there" waiting for us if we make the effort to look for those friends who need us just as we need them. As someone put it, "A stranger is a good friend I haven't met yet."

Grief makes us grow, whether we want to or not! Frankl says, "That which does not kill us makes us stronger." If our grief does not kill our spirit and make us bitter, it makes us stronger and more compassionate.

An article about Clark Gable said, "Friends detected an unexpected gentleness in Clark Gable after Carole Lombard was killed that hadn't been there before." A disciplined woman in her eighties told me she had never been depressed in her life until her husband died, and then her own depression made her understand and sympathize with others who were depressed. Daniel Considine wrote: "By wanting sympathy and not getting it, we learn by experience how to sympathize with others. No one is so well able to give sympathy as one who has known the want of it; one who wishes to save others from having to drink the cup from which he himself has deeply drunk" (Confidence in God).

Having faced tragedy ourselves, we become aware of the pain of those around us who are facing their dark nights of the soul. Being ourselves familiar with the struggle involved in coping with adversity, we admire and sympathize with other people in tragic circumstances who accept —without bitterness—the things they cannot change and make the most of what life holds for them.

I probably never will be able to accept the things I cannot change without a trace of bitterness. I suppose I'll always wrestle with anger and frustration over the unfairness of life, and feel sorry for myself occasionally when a problem comes up I have to handle all by myself; but I'll never again let envy and bitterness destroy my capacity to enjoy people and life.

I thank God I can enjoy people and life again, and that I came through my hell intact. I feel like myself again, but I'll never forget what it was like when I was not myself at all—when I was a stranger to myself, standing on the sidelines, watching other people live. I am no longer a stranger to myself, but, paradoxically, I am a *different* person, because of what I have experienced and what I have learned through grief. I hope to change into a still more "different" me in the years to come, as I experience more of life's joys and sorrows and try to learn from them.

I am no longer afraid of growing old, with all of its heartaches, because I have already surmounted the insurmountable—with the help of others and a higher power. And I know now that no matter what trials lie ahead for me, there will always be people and that higher power to come to my rescue with their love again, who will always be there to help me laugh and to help me cry; to help me live and to help me die.

I wish reading this book could quickly cure you of your grief and make you happy; but of course it can't. *You must cure yourself.* You can do it, but it won't be easy. It will take time, *patience with yourself,* and perseverance. Grief and depression are normal, healthy emotions for anyone in difficult circumstances; but don't let them become a way of life for you *for any reason*.

Dale Carnegie said he reread his own books because he forgot what he had written. When I get bogged down about my situation and need to straighten out my thinking again, I reread the parts of this book that apply to the problem at hand; and I suggest that you do the same.

On your darkest days, remember that no one can appreciate the heights who has not been to the depths—which makes you and me candidates for experiencing the sublime!

Further Reading

I have found the following books, most of which I mention or quote from in the preceding chapters, helpful to me:

CONSIDINE, DANIEL, *Confidence in God* (Sign: Union City, N.J. 1977).

CRAVENS, MARGARET, *I Heard the Owl Call My Name* (New York: Doubleday, 1973).

FRANKL, VIKTOR, *Man's Search for Meaning* (Boston: Beacon Press, 1963).

GINOTT, HAIM, *Between Parent and Child* (New York: Macmillan, 1965).

GRAY, MADELINE, *The Changing Years* (New York: New American Library 1973).

HULME, WILLIAM E., *Creative Loneliness* (Augsburg Publishing House 1977).

JAUNCEY, JAMES H., *Above Ourselves* (Grand Rapids: Zondervan 1964).

LIEBMAN, JOSHUA L., *Peace of Mind* (New York: Simon and Schuster 1965).

MALTZ, MAXWELL, *Psycho-Cybernetics* (Englewood Cliffs: Prentice-Hall, 1960).

NEWMAN, MILDRED, and BERNARD BERKOWITZ, *How to Be Your Own Best Friend* (New York: Random House 1971).

QUOIST, MICHEL, *The Meaning of Success* (Notre Dame: Fides-Claretian 1963).

VAN COEVERING, VIRGINIA ROGERS, "An Exploratory Study of Middle-aged and Older Widows to Investigate Those Variables Which Differentiate High and Low Life Satisfaction" (diss., Wayne University 1973).

WESTBERG, GRANGER E., *Good Grief* (Philadelphia: Fortress 1962).